To: Tammy

Peace
Bill '32

THE POA DEFENSE

An Eyewitness Narrative of the Pacific Ocean Area Events of World War II

by

Lieutenant Colonel William Cazy Smith

SHELBY HOUSE

1989

Shelby House
1407 Union Avenue
401 Mid-Memphis Tower
Memphis, Tennessee 38104

ISBN 0-942-179-72-5

Typography by Patterson Publications, Inc.

Table of Contents

In Memory of My Mother
Roxie McCown Smith

She endured the agony of having five sons in World War II who fought around the world from the steaming jungles of New Guinea to the Battle of the Bulge. She lived long enough to see each of them return home, and then became the lone family casualty. She died December 18, 1952, at the age of seventy from natural causes brought on by stress and long suffering during the war.

Preface

When I was discharged from the Army after World War II, I knew I had to put the years of war and their turmoil behind me before I could get on with a normal life. With the help of family, friends, and the blessings of time, I managed to bury the war years and all their ugliness somewhere in the past. Now after forty-two years I find myself delving back into the dark recesses of time for those long, buried memories to write this book.

At first the memories of suffering, agony, and horror would overwhelm me, and I could only write for short periods of time without a long rest. But gradually I built up a toughness to the emotions these memories rekindled and was able to record the events as I remembered them. During this process of collecting memories I found a certain healing began to take place. Soon I almost welcomed the recall of old faces, places and events.

Those years would have been much easier left buried, but a number of factors prompted me to record my experiences in World War II. Among them was my feeling that many books written about the war are fiction and fail to relate the reality of how it was to live war day by day. Others are so careful to stick to the historical facts that they become boring and hard to read. I believe future generations will benefit more if they have both historical and personal material to choose from when they read about the war. I hope I have succeeded in writing an account that is both interesting and factual.

I received encouragement from a number of young officers at the Pentagon, the Pearl Harbor Survivors' Association, Mississippi State University, and from friends. I was also inspired to complete this book by a new generation of young people who seem to have a never-ending thirst for more firsthand knowledge of our military history.

Finally, I was seeking the best way to preserve a permanent

record of my broad experiences in the Pacific Area of World War II, and because of the length of the project, a book seemed the best method.

The experiences as related here are based on actual happenings, observations and reflections—most of which are recorded from memory and are substantiated by numerous documents and photographs.

Veterans are tortured the rest of their lives with memories of war and its horror. Once being exposed to war it is painfully clear that all wars are senseless and follow a familiar pattern in their conception.

I recall that the events leading up to the Vietnam War in early 1960 followed the well known pattern perfectly. We provoked the little man—he answered our challenge with threats from his small naval forces—we shot back and the war was on. I was so disturbed by this action that I was reluctant to admit I had ever been in the military service.

The new generation and our national leaders were too busy to look at the past for clues as to how wrong they were in these actions that once again put our young men on the battle field. Preparedness, restraint and diplomacy are key words for avoiding war. President "Teddy" Roosevelt said it first, although he used different words.

A few years after world War II was over I learned of the death of General Burgin. Also, Major John Hart, a member or our Antiaircraft Artillery staff, Pacific Ocean Areas, who died in Korea during that war. According to the reports I received, they both died by their own hand. I think of them as belated casualties of war. In my appraisal every person who fights in a war is a casualty and should be awarded the Purple Heart. In a broader interpretation I contend the entire nation is also a casualty. Wounds to the flesh usually heal quickly, but wounds to the soul heal slowly, if ever they heal at all.

Introduction

The Pacific Ocean Area is the largest ocean area in the world, claiming one half of the earth's water surface. Divided by the equator into the North and South Pacific it covers an area of seventy million square miles or one third of the earth's total area. The greatest known depth is 36,520 feet and is located in the Marianas Trench, known as the "Vitiaz Deep." The water pressure on the floor is seven tons per square inch; yet, life exists at this great depth. The ocean derived its name from the Latin word "pacificus" which means peaceful, calm, or tranquil.

Before July 1941, my knowledge of this area was limited. When I thought of the Pacific, I usually imagined such things as grass skirts, flying fish, and vast blue water, speckled with small tropical islands. These images were fed by such movies as "The Road to Rio" with Bob Hope, Bing Crosby and Dorothy Lamour. I had a wistful desire to see what lay beyond the horizon in that fabled land of palm-shrouded isles.

But far from a peaceful island paradise, these islands during World War II were bastions of hell. The Japanese were dug-in on the white, sandy beaches; snipers perched in the tops of palm trees; and gun emplacements were hidden in every knoll. They fought from these fortified positions with a tenacity never before experienced by the American fighting man. The enemy was fanatic and chose death over surrender and dishonor.

It was a cockfight from the beginning for Allied ground forces in the war with Japan. This conflict, with its fast moving land, sea, and air armament, could hardly be compared to that experienced by the doughboy in the muddy trenches of Europe during World War I. Their battles were fought, for the most part, by the book, and they knew they had to move from one trench to the next until the ground was won. In the Pacific, each island was an operation within itself, and each operation influenced our strategy for the next island assault. The topography and size of each island, plus the lessons learned from previous landings were used as a blueprint for the next battle.

The Navy and Air Force softened up the areas to be invaded with concentrated bombardment and transported Army and Marine ground forces to the landing beaches. Each invasion force was custom-built, according to the needs necessary to take and garrison the new base. It was a joint effort of all U. S. military forces at hand, with the primary mission of the Navy and Air Force being to protect shipping lanes; necessitating the never-ending fight for supremacy of the air and seas.

In July 1941, seven months after being called to active duty in the United States Army, I was transferred to the Hawaiian Department and sailed from San Francisco aboard the *USS President Coolidge*, a luxury liner on lease to the maritime service. For the next forty-six months my domain was the Pacific area.

The last thirty months of this time my assignment was Chief Antiaircraft Artillery Staff Officer of the area, which eventually became "Headquarters, United States Army Forces Pacific Ocean Areas." We were responsible for all areas within a boundary on the south roughly following the equator and a boundary on the north to include all Pacific Ocean Areas (POA). Also included were all of Japan, the Philippines, and other territories therein. The Naval arm of POA was responsible for all water areas in this hemisphere.

I was fortunate to have served with such great men as Admiral Chester W. Nimitz, who was the Commander in Chief of all the armed forces in the area, and Lt. General Robert C. Richardson, the Commanding Officer of the Army Component of POA. The Southwest Pacific area was under the command of General Douglas A. MacArthur.

My staff assignment was interesting but demanding. Most of my time was spent on the beautiful island of Oahu, Hawaii. My primary duty was to assure maximum efficiency in the employment of antiaircraft units used in static and assault landing operations. Not only was I responsible for the preliminary design of the artillery needed to defend the new bases, but also for the deployment of the necessary units to do the job.

I spent long periods of time in forward areas inspecting island defenses, and I participated in two assault landings as an observer. I was responsible for writing official reports of these operations and of my inspection trips to the islands. There were many short observation trips aboard aircraft carriers and practice dive bombing trips with Navy pilots which were a welcome break in the routine.

During my travels I catalogued important information about the terra, fauna, and flora of our battleground. Most of the smaller islands fell in the category of coral atolls, while larger ones were volcanic in nature. The atolls lie low in the water and when aboard ship, the first thing that can be seen is what appears to be a long, aligned grove of coconut trees emerging from the sea. As the ships draw closer a narrow white band of coral is visible, which is the support base for the soil and trees. Many of these islands looked like wedding rings with a beautiful lagoon inside the loop.

All the islands tactically favored the defender who had converted them into fortresses. The volcanic islands were the most treacherous. They offered defensive advantages such as altitude, natural caves, and rugged terrain. The allied forces could not rely on surprise, cover, or concealment to get safely on the beaches. In fact most of our casualties occurred in the distance traveled from the ship across the treacherous reef to the beach. During this time the landing crafts were most vulnerable to the intense barrage of shelling from the defenders. Only after a foothold was established on the beaches did the going become less hazardous.

The invasion forces may have faced the tactical and strategical problems of taking their assigned targets, but an even larger logistical problem fell to the Naval Forces responsible for keeping thousands of miles of supply lines open. If they failed in this task, all related operations would fail, regardless of how superior their strength.

LIST OF ILLUSTRATIONS

Figure 1. Diagram: Routes of Japanese Attack in Oahu, December 7, 1941. The planes that hit Wheeler Field deployed from the group at 07:40 A.M. North of Oahu and arrived on target at 07:50 A.M. Others in the group proceeded to Pearl Harbor arriving there at 07:55 A.M. [Permission to reprint this graphic is gratefully acknowledged from Headquarters Hickham field command, Oahu, Hawaii.]

Figure 2. News Release: United States Air Force casualty and damage list, December 7, 1941. [author's collection]

Figure 3. Photo: Wheeler Field, adjacent to Schofield Barracks, Oahu, during Japanese attack, December 7, 1941. Runways are in background. Captain Smith's 98th AAA Battery traversed the street from right to left on the near side of the prominent white building enroute to its battle position at the end of the runway. Tent bivouac near the center white building was completely demolished but no one was in the tents at the moment, thereby escaping great loss of life. [Permission to reprint this photograph is gratefully acknowledged from Headquarters Wheeler field command, Oahu, Hawaii.]

Figure 4. Photo: Captain William Cazy Smith (left) with Lt. Col. Edward Farnsworth (right) making his first inspection of AAA unit after assignment to artillery staff position. Captain Tigrett Battery Commander (center). Col. Farnsworth was promoted to a command position elsewhere and was replaced by Captain Smith on the Artillery Staff. The Colt 45 service revolver worn by Captain Smith was in service during WW I and given to him by the widow of Lt. Stiner, a cavalry officer. Many officers for sentimental purposes prefer to use their own gun. Note camouflage net overhead. [author's collection]

Figure 5. Photo: Headquarters staff, Hawaiian artillery command. Front row (left to right) Major General Henry T. Burgin, Colonel E. V. Holmes, Lt. Colonel Boldt, Lt. Col. Nick Carter. (Back row) Major Cox, Major John Taylor, Major William Cazy Smith, Captain Herbert Hucks. This organization was absorbed, for the most part, by the Pacific Ocean Areas command after reorganization prior to our thrust into the Central Pacific Area. [author's collection]

Figure 6. Photo: Hawaiian artillery staff with their guests seated at the solid monkey pod banquet table in the Henry Fagin Mansion, Honolulu, Hawaii. (clockwise) Major Cox, Lt. Colonel William Cazy Smith, Lt. Colonel Robert Ferguson, Colonel E.V. Holmes, Major General Henry T. Burgin, Lt. Colonel Boldt, Mr. Henry T. Fagin, Jr., Lt. Colonel Nick Carter, Major Henry Taylor, Captain Herbert Hucks. Colonel Ferguson, a former member of the staff, was visiting. At this time he was G-2 Seventh Infantry Division. Having participated in the Attu invasion, the division was on Oahu staging for action in the South Pacific. [author's collection]

Figure 7. Document: Letter from Major General Henry T. Burgin to Major William Cazy Smith December 5, 1943 while he was attending an AAA refresher course at Camp Davis, NC. [author's collection]

Figure 8. Membership of Air Defense Control Center Board, Pacific Ocean Areas command. This board was formed in an attempt to improve the use of our air defense facilities in the defense of island bases, and during assault operations. Fire against enemy aircraft was controlled from aboard ship during the assault phase. In theory, this was not a complicated operation for the naval air force and the AAA, but in fact never seemed to work very well. Then, too, most large assault units had a limited number of antiaircraft weapons in their organizations. It was almost impossible to control the status of fire for these weapons; thus when any plane flew low over the assault area pandemonium was inevitable. The personnel of the combat units had little or no plane identification training, so on many occasions they fired at our own planes. [author's collection]

Figure 9. Map of Saipan

Figures 10-17. Document: Official observer's report on preparation for the movement of Task force tree (Bakers Island) a part of the Tarawa assault by Lt. Col. William Cazy Smith Dated 20 September, 1943. [author's collection]

Figures 18-26. Document: Official observer's report of the Saipan operation By Lt. Col. William Cazy Smith, dated 7 July, 1944. [author's collection]

Figure 27. Photo: Aerial photo (June 15, 1944) of Saipan assault. Includes first two waves of landing vessels and breakers over coral reef. Shore line lower right is out of picture view. Smoke in the area is from aerial bombardment minutes earlier and gun fire from landing crafts. Breakers over reef are about two hundred yards off shore and parallel to it. The command ship has not yet entered the picture upper left. It initially led the way but fell back to the rear and anchored about five hundred years from the shore well within range of Japanese heavy machine gun fire. [Permission to reprint this photograph is gratefully acknowledged from the National Archives, Washington. D.C.]

• An Eyewitness Account •

Figure 28. Photo: First wave action on the landing beaches of Saipan June 15, 1944. Marines tied down on beach waiting for other troops to clear out fire from pill boxes. Two normal ways to knock out the pill box: (1) fire high explosive penetrating shells into frontal vents, (2) approach pill box from blind side and attack with grenades and flame thrower; or a combination of both may be used. Defilade from the slightly elevated shore line gave them protection from most of the rifle and machinegun fire but not artillery fire. At this site artillery fire was intermittent. Thought the Japanese defense on Saipan was formidable, it was impossible for them to cover the entire shoreline with block houses and artillery fire; yet, artillery fire can be adjusted or moved to cover many areas. The softening up attack by planes and warships helped, but could not completely neutralize their fire. Weak and strong points of a defense are common situations. One does not doggedly push forward in the face of strong resistance. You wait for forces on your flanks who are better able to advance to neutralize the heavy threat in your sector. [Permission to reprint this photograph is gratefully acknowledged from the National Archives, Washington. D.C.]

Figure 29. Photo: Tank now on Perilous Reef is first to hit the beach. [Permission to reprint this photograph is gratefully acknowledged from the National Archives, Washington. D.C.]

Figure 30. Photo: Under enemy fire. [Permission to reprint this photograph is gratefully acknowledged from the National Archives, Washington. D.C.]

Figure 31. Photo: Tank shields marines as they cautiously move forward. [Permission to reprint this photograph is gratefully acknowledged from the National Archives, Washington. D.C.]

Figure 32. Photo: Action on Red Beach. [Permission to reprint this photograph is gratefully acknowledged from the National Archives, Washington. D.C.]

Figure 33. Photo: Saipan, June 1944. Marine throws grenade at Japanese holed up in cave. [Permission to reprint this photograph is gratefully acknowledged from the National Archives, Washington. D.C.]

Figure 34. Photo: Marine hurling grenade in attack on Japanese strong point. [Permission to reprint this photograph is gratefully acknowledged from the National Archives, Washington. D.C.]

Figure 35. Photo: Marine guarding bodies of slain comrades in arms. Typical bunker in background. [Permission to reprint this photograph is gratefully acknowledged form the National Archives, Washington. D.C.]

Figure 36. Photo: Garapan, Saipan under siege June, 1944. Garapan was completely demolished because the Japanese infantry entrenched themselves en masse in the entire city. Chalon Kanoa received only slight damage in our landing because the Japanese did not commit their infantry there, depending on artillery and automatic weapons in fixed defensive positions. [Permission to reprint this photograph is gratefully acknowledged from the National Archives, Washington. D.C.]

Figure 37. Photo: Saipan, June 1944. Aftermath of Japanese counter thrust in marsh area between Chalon Kanoa and high ground. About 175 Japanese participated in this suicidal attack. Marines were well set up for the expected attack and mowed them down while receiving slight casualties. [Permission to reprint this photograph is gratefully acknowledged form the National Archives, Washington. D.C.]

• An Eyewitness Account •

Figure 38. Photo: Saipan June 15, 1944. LST beached on coral reef after discharge of attack personnel and armament. [Permission to reprint this photograph is gratefully acknowledged from the National Archives, Washington. D.C.]

Figure 39. Photo: Saipan, June, 1944. Replacement troops wading ashore from beached LSTs some time after the beach was secure. [Permission to reprint this photograph is gratefully acknowledged from the National Archives, Washington. D.C.]

Figure 40. Photo: Saipan, June, 1944. Amplifiers set up to broadcast instructions to civilians and military who may or may not be in our custody. [Permission to reprint this photograph is gratefully acknowledged from the National Archives, Washington. D.C.]

Figure 41. Photo: Marines pinned down on landing Iwo Jima beach. [Permission to reprint this photograph is gratefully acknowledged from the National Archives, Washington. D.C.]

Figure 42. Photo: Iwo Jima, February 1945. Portable flame thrower in action. It was being used to snuff out any Japanese in the bunker that might remain a threat. Some flame throwers are mounted on tanks for use against bunkers where the danger is greater and time is of the essence. [Permission to reprint this photograph is gratefully acknowledged form the National Archives, Washington. D.C.]

Figure 43. Photo: Aftermath of Iwo Jima assault February 19, 1945. Marines lost 5,563 dead and 17,343 wounded. Gasoline drums were Japanese (Marines used five gallon cans to transport gasoline during a landing) and part of a bizarre plan to set fire to the beach at the most strategic moment. For some unknown reason they did not execute this scheme. [Permission to reprint this photograph is gratefully acknowledged from the National Archives, Washington. D.C.]

Figures 44-46. Document: Letter of instructions from admiral Chester W. Nimitz to area commanders announcing the forthcoming operational plans for occupation of Okinawa, Ryuku islands. This instrument was handed to, among others, all staff personnel with responsibility to design a portion of the landing and garrison forces in the assault. This was the last such instrument issued during the war with Japan. As in all previous assaults it was the responsibility of Lt. Col. William Cazy Smith to design the AAA Defense plan for the occasion. No instruction other than this and similar documents were needed for preparation of these plans. He designed them far ahead of their current or potential need. [author's collection]

Figures 47-50. Document: Letter of commendation to AAA units 97th AAA Group (loaned to the Southwest Pacific Command by Pacific Ocean Areas Command) by General Douglas MacArthur with inclosure and indorsement. [author's collection]

Figure 51-52. Document: Letter dated 20 November, 1944 from HQ Garrison Force, Saipan with information on employment of AAA. [author's collection]

Figure 53. Newspaper Clipping: "Our Smith Family Goes to War" which appeared in *The Broadcaster* published by the students of Whitehaven, Tennessee High School, and was later reprinted by the *Herald* of Collierville, Tennessee. [author's collection]

Figure 54. Photo: Typical cave in Saipan. [author's collection]

Figure 55. Photo: Block house on Garapan beach now being used to store sail surfing equipment. [author's collection]

Figure 56. Photo: Col. Smith at the site of the Banzai attack near Tanapag, Saipan. Note the bullet holes in the sign left by vandals. [author's collection]

Figure 57. Photo: Site of Japanese prison where downed American airmen were imprisoned on Saipan. Local legend has it that Amelia Earhart was kept here temporarily. [author's collection]

Figure 58. Photo: Suicide Cliff at Lagua Katan Point (most northern point on Saipan) where thousands of Japanese civilians committed suicide. [author's collection]

Figure 59. Photo: Col. Smith at grave side of guide's sister killed by Naval gunfire during the battle for Saipan. [author's collection]

Figure 60. Photo: Guide points out to Col. Smith Disabled Tank on Red Beach Saipan. [author's collection]

Figure 61. Photo: Col. Smith and his wife, Frances, on Blue Beach, Saipan, where he came ashore with the Marines, June 16, 1944. [author's collection]

1

THE DAY THE WATERS STOOD STILL

It was early afternoon, April 14, 1944, almost three years after I set sail from San Francisco for Hawaii, and twenty-nine months since the attack on Pearl Harbor. Our location was approximately 6000 miles west of San Francisco, and 50 miles northeast of Saipan. All five hundred ships in our convoy had stopped dead in the water. The resulting silence, after living so many days with the deafening noise of the convoy, was eerie and the mirror calm water added to the sense of foreboding.

The purpose of this stop was to shift personnel from one ship to another in preparation for an assault on the west shore of Saipan the next morning. I was observer aboard the command ship and I was to write an operational report on all facets directly or indirectly affecting the antiaircraft artillery during the attack.

The young marines and sailors who wandered calmly around on deck displayed no outward signs that they were prepared to board the waiting landing crafts and go into battle in a few short hours. Some were getting haircuts on the open deck, some were laughing and jostling each other, still others were sitting quietly writing letters, reading, or meditating. But just under this display of nonchalance I knew there was an aura of fear and uncertainty, because I felt it myself.

Soon we were under way again and by night were sailing past Saipan on the north to get in position for the attack to take place from the west along a line containing the town of Chalan Kanoa. For several days our carrier-based planes had maintained a constant bombardment of the island, and a blockade had been set up by our ships. On the eve of the attack, large Naval warships had moved close to the island to bombard the shoreline areas. The island was kept almost constantly lit by flares. From aboard our command ship, we observed this spectacle as though we were watching a display of fireworks.

Our day would officially start at 4:30 a.m. with a breakfast of steak and eggs. This would be the last meal for thousands of the young Marines and sailors aboard who were about to take their first step into a journey through hell.

Until that evening our movement from Pearl Harbor had not been unlike a peacetime maneuver. As I stood on deck watching the fireworks, I began to reflect on my past. I was haunted by thoughts of, "How did I get here? What series of events led me to this spot at this point in my life? Was I an unfortunate victim of fate or had my life followed a pattern which made this moment inevitable?" As I looked around, my eyes focused on other individuals with the same serious questions in mind. Why was this or that person here? Whose lot would it be to pay the supreme price? Was it necessary that we bear the cross of a fallen comrade? I thought about their loved ones—mothers, fathers, brothers, sisters, wives, and children. These thoughts made me realize my name was on the list also. I was fifty miles off the island of Saipan gazing into the black ocean from the deck of a troopship, wondering if I would be one of the casualties. In those moments I realized I was no different from the thousands who had gone into battle before me. They too must have used the quiet time on the eve of battle, not for planning the future but for remembering the past. How did I get from the quiet isolation of Owl Creek, Mississippi, to the deck of a U.S. war ship in the Pacific? I sighed as my mind took me back in time.

I was the third son and seventh child in a family of fourteen and was fortunate indeed to have had loving, caring, hard working parents. My father, a strict disciplinarian, spared the rod, but we feared his reprimands more than the peach tree switch our mother often used. Even though my parents were strict, their discipline was well balanced with love, giving us a solid basis for a happy childhood.

I have many fond memories of the four and one-half years I spent at Mount Zion School, a two-room white clapboard structure with grades one through five occupying one room and grades six through eight in the other. Two teachers were assigned to the school, one for each room.

During these early years, I developed a strong interest in insects and spent many hours watching them. I was most fascinated by ants and their ability to construct tunnels and roads. By following their example, I discovered I had a natural talent for building miniature roads and bridges. I made a make believe wagon using empty spools to push along the roads and spent many happy hours at this pastime. These homemade toys, bridges and roads were the beginning of a growing interest in engineering, which eventually became my major in college.

In December 1920, my family moved from our home located one mile west of Faulkner, Mississippi to a farm on Owl Creek, four miles east of Ripley, Mississippi. This move put me in Parks Chapel, a one-room, one-teacher school. I graduated from the eighth grade there and moved on to Mississippi High School in Ripley. The quality of instruction at Ripley High was excellent, but the curriculum did not measure up to the standards of most schools in the state. This was a pronounced disadvantage for graduates, such as myself, who chose to go on to college.

After school and on weekends, I worked at a local filling station and kept books for the local Standard Oil Company distributor. By September 1928, I had saved four hundred dollars, enough to pay for my freshman year at Mississippi Agricultural and Mechanical College.

Bobby Hines, my employer at the Ripley Service Station, and a graduate of Mississippi A & M, had recommended the college to me. Also A & M had a good scholastic standing, and was located close to my home. It didn't matter that it was known as a poor man's cow college with the lowest possible tuition.

College opened up a new world for me. Though most of my rural life I was privileged by north Mississippi hill country standards, I was not prepared for the changes that would take place in my living conditions. My entire surrounding had changed from the food I ate to the bed I slept in. But the biggest change for me was to experience inside plumbing and electric lights.

Most students lived in the large quadrangle, four-story dormitory and ate in the adjoining cafeteria. Although we had fraternities, there were no fraternity houses. Each dormitory room contained a three-tier cot, a study table with chairs, and a lavatory. A bathroom was shared by thirty students. At this time all the students were male. The college went coeducational during my junior year, but all the female students lived off campus.

The absence of girls in an all-boys school only enhances one's desire to be in their company. On Sundays the few boys who were fortunate enough to have a date would stroll around the campus which made the other students envious. No wonder the song "Sweethearts on Parade" was popular at this time. Hearing it only accentuated our desires.

For those without female companionship, a shanty town in Starkville inhabited by black prostitutes provided a sexual outlet. On one occasion I agreed to visit the area with a fellow student but refused to participate in the activities, even though he offered to pay the two dollar fee. I vividly recall this episode and the light-hearted kidding I received from my colleagues on our way back to the campus.

Unless a student had made his own arrangements, college officials assigned roommates. Since I didn't know anyone, I waited to be assigned a roommate and was lucky to be teamed with Walter Lee Woods. He was a wonderful person from a fine family, and I liked him at once. Sharing space with Lee proved to be a rewarding experience. Being the son of a Gulfport,

• The POA Defense •

Mississippi judge, Lee's childhood had been more refined than mine, and I learned a lot from him. I will always be grateful for the culture I absorbed from him. Lee was an affable, gentle person who was loved by everyone who knew him. In later years Lee became Public Representative for Promotion of Industry in the State of Mississippi.

Science, agriculture, and engineering were part of the predetermined schedule of studies for the first two years at Mississippi A & M. In fact, after enrollment and selection of a specialty, about the only option a student had was in the selection of his instructors.

Campus life was very disciplined, and I soon fell into the routine. At 9:30 p.m. the bugle call to quarters was sounded, and shortly thereafter an inspector came by to verify our presence in our rooms. Most of us used this time for studying and preparing for the next day. No loud noise was permitted after taps was sounded at 11:00 p.m. and this usually signaled the end of our day.

There were many rules covering other areas of activity and an infraction drew the prescribed demerits. To go beyond the limit in demerits resulted in expulsion from college. I do not recall receiving any demerits. In fact the only reprimand I received was while I was still in high school when an airplane landed in a field nearby during lunch time, and I ran down to get a closer look. As a result, I was late getting back to my desk.

High school did not prepare me for the study assignments in college where ten times as much material was assigned. I had more responsibility for studying and no parent or sibling to help or urge me to get my assignments done. I did not have a natural talent for the literary arts, so some subjects were very difficult for me. I was also troubled by an inability to develop good study habits. Because of this I had to work twice as hard as my roommate just to maintain a passing grade. Hard work and determination paid off and by my senior year, I excelled in many subjects.

• An Eyewitness Account •

By today's standards the recreational facilities, at Mississippi A & M were meager, but they exceeded anything I had known in my pre-college days. We did not have a gymnasium, and there were no intramural activities other than the college teams sponsored by the athletic department.

Track was my choice for sport participation as it did not require any special talent. My best performances were in the broad jump and mile race. Although, I did not make the team, I supported it by attending track meets.

Competition with other colleges in football, baseball, and track drew almost one hundred percent attendance from the student body. Rivalry was intense, and the fans were noisy in their team support. Basketball was played on an outdoor court, and as a result the games were not as well attended by the students.

Activities by the fraternities were more or less confined to formal dances, but many of us could not afford this luxury. We found other ways to spend our idle time such as strolling down the boulevard to Starkville and patronizing their one, and only, movie theater.

Sports and limited social activities helped me settle into a college routine and soon reflected favorably on my studies. I was very pleased with my continued improvement in my scholastic standing during my senior year but was discouraged by the decline in job opportunities for engineering students. In earlier years almost all of the engineering students had jobs waiting, but not one of our 1932 graduates left college with a job waiting in the profession he was trained and educated for.

In fact, in some cases my business degree was a liability in my search for employment. Even my offer to work for free on a trial basis at the Memphis Light, Gas and Water Company was rejected. The president of the company was very sympathetic during our conference but didn't have an available position. Although my job situation did continue to improve, partly due to

• The POA Defense •

President Roosevelt's New Deal, I never had an opportunity to follow an engineering profession.

My introduction to the military came while I was in college through the Reserve Officer Training Corps (ROTC).

An act of Congress in 1862, known as the Morrill Act, granted each state thirty thousand acres of land for each member it had in Congress. Ninety percent of the gross proceeds from the land was used to endow colleges teaching agricultural and mechanical arts. Mississippi A & M was one of these land grant colleges, and it was mandatory that all students take reserve officer training for the first two years. The second two years this training was elective. In the third and fourth years, ROTC provided advanced study in military science. Those who successfully completed the entire course in ROTC received a commission as Second Lieutenant in the United States Army Reserve, and engineering graduates were assigned to the Coast Artillery Corps.

The Army paid ROTC students in advanced training nine dollars per month, plus a small uniform allowance. Although this amount was small, it is doubtful that some of us could have continued in school without these meager funds. My decision to take advanced studies in military science and tactics was influenced by these funds and by the handsome ROTC uniform which proved to be an automatic status symbol.

Military science and tactics covered a broad range of subjects and included everything from personal hygiene to housekeeping, astronomy, and medicine. Its broad scope in nature and my natural curiosity about how things work made military science and tactics one of my favorite subjects.

The organization of the ROTC was somewhat like the regular Army with squads, platoons, companies, battalions, and regiments. Each cadet had his assigned position in the unit, and advanced students were given leadership assignments. Training other than academics included manual of arms, drill routines and

27

marching. Each cadet had his own rifle and was responsible for keeping it clean. Advanced students were classified as officers and each had his own saber he wore for drills.

Our Saturday morning parades were exciting and invigorating. The echoing of commands across the parade ground, the rhythmic sound of 'Manual of Arms', the command 'Sound Off' to the band, the stimulus of discipline, the excitement of anticipation, the beautiful marching music, and the competitive 'March In Review' made this event the highlight of our week. To this day my adrenaline surges when I hear John Phillip Sousa's 'Stars and Stripes Forever'.

In addition to our regular school training, we were required to participate in one six-week summer training camp at the end of our junior year. Our unit was assigned to Fort Barancas in Pensacola, Florida. The entire six weeks was devoted to training and firing some of the large seacoast guns. These sixteen-inch bore guns were installed in permanent positions along the coastline on Santa Rosa Island across from our camp on Pensacola Bay. Their purpose was to defend the Pensacola harbor. The projectiles weighed approximately one thousand pounds with a range of about fifteen miles. This was during the summer of 1931 and such guns were nearing the end of their role in national defense. Some time later the ammunition for these guns was purportedly sold to the Japanese government for its salvage value. After the Japanese bombing of Pearl Harbor on December 7, 1941, there were news reports stating that some of the shells were used as bombs by the attacking airplanes. However, I was there and knew of no official information that would substantiate this claim.

I enjoyed every moment of my four years of military training and took great pride in being a part of our national defense. The thought never occurred to me during these carefree years that I would later give five of the most vital years of my life in the defense of my country.

• The POA Defense •

I continued my studies in military science and tactics by correspondence after my graduation in 1932. These correspondence courses were conducted by the War Department and involved more field training. Each summer, whenever government funds were available, I was ordered to two weeks active duty at a military establishment. I usually reported to a different post in the southeast part of the United States each year. For this service I was paid a salary equal to the salary paid a regular career officer in my rank and length of service. Participation in this training was necessary for continued status as a reserve officer and advancement in grade.

In the spotlight of this temporary duty was the display of our most modern weaponry, the demonstration of its capabilities and the latest weapons improvement. For the AAA the greatest change was the semi-mobile, three-inch bore gun which replaced the old fixed mount weapons. The gun could be towed by a truck to the desired location where four fold-out arms would replace the wheels. The gun could be made ready to fire in only a few minutes.

These demonstrations were frequently attended by VIPs and occasionally by Franklin D. Roosevelt, then President of the United States. The leaders of our military forces went to great lengths to publicize the invincibility of our armed forces and to promote the Army's image during these displays.

In September 1935, I volunteered for a six month period of duty with the United States Army to participate in the administration of the Civilian Conservation Corps (CCC). This brainchild of President Franklin D. Roosevelt was developed to give employment and schooling to young men. The Corps was used to improve the nation's parks and was under the direction of the Forest Service. The Smoky Mountain National Park in Tremont, Tennessee, was the site of my first camp. Every service necessary to maintain and administer the camp was provided by the Army.

29

• An Eyewitness Account •

The Army also made the work details available to the Forest Service for use as the need arose. In the Smoky Mountains, these work details were used to construct scenic trails.

The camp staff consisted of two reserve line officers, one reserve officer medical doctor, and one civilian educational advisor. The medical doctor usually served two or more camps.

During the evenings, the education advisor conducted classes covering a broad range of subjects such as reading, writing, arithmetic, and handicraft. Since many of the camp members could neither read nor write, teaching them these basic skills was given a high priority. It was a gratifying experience to see the proud look on a young man's face when he wrote his very first letter home to his mother.

I served two and one-half years in this service and enjoyed it immensely. We always had a break of about a month between each tour to accommodate each new group of officers participating in the program.

Later I served in camps at Cherokee National Forest in Tennessee; Cumberland Ridge, Tennessee; William B. Bankhead National Forest, Alabama; Sequoia National Park, California, and Griffith Park, Los Angeles, California. Each location was different and had its own unique attraction. For example, the Sequoia National Park had its giant, majestic Sequoia trees, scenic views, and an abundance of wild life.

At Griffith Park, our camp was near the Walt Disney and other movie studios and the home of Bette Davis. We all enjoyed being in the company of the people who brought movies to life; in fact, most of the people I met while I was there worked with the studios. Adjacent to camp and only a few feet from my quarters was a bridle trail. Frequently a movie star using the trail would detour through our camp and stop to chat with some of the men. There were even rumors that on occasions a night riding Lady Godiva was seen riding on the trail.

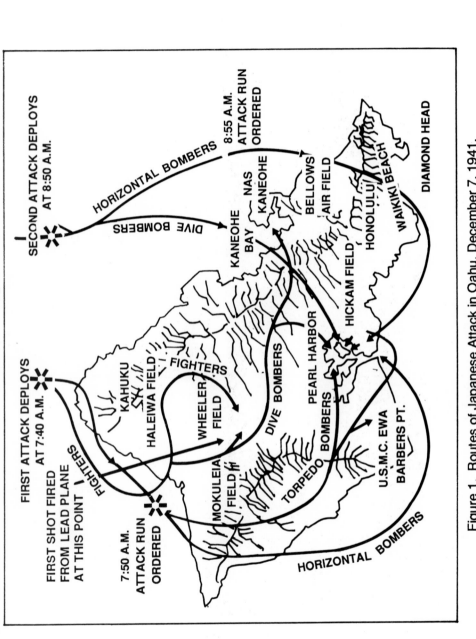

Figure 1. Routes of Japanese Attack in Oahu, December 7, 1941.

NEWS RELEASE
UNITED STATES AIR FORCE

Office of Informatinn, 6486th Air Base Wing (PACAFBASECOM), Hickam AFB, Hawaii
Release No. 66715   Date: January 10, 1967   Phone: 443367

DECEMBER 7th, 1941

HAWAIIAN AIR FORCE — CASUALTIES AND DAMAGE

(total Strength as of November 30, 1941: 754 Officers, 6,706 Enlisted Men,= 7,460)

CASUALTIES	KILLED	MISSING	WOUNDED	
Hickam	121	37	274	
Wheeler	37	6	53	
Bellows	5	0	9	
Total	163	43	336	= 542

PLANES

Out of a total of 231 aircraft of Hawaiian Air Force, 64 were destroyed and not more than 79 left usable:

	On Hand	After Attack	Usable
B-17D	12	8	4
B-18A	33	21	11
A-20A	12	10	5
P-40C	12	7	2
P-40B	87	50	25
P-36A	39	35	16
Total	209 *	131	63

* Plus an assortment of observation, training, and attack planes, including 14, P-26's.

Figure 2. News Release: December 7, 1941.

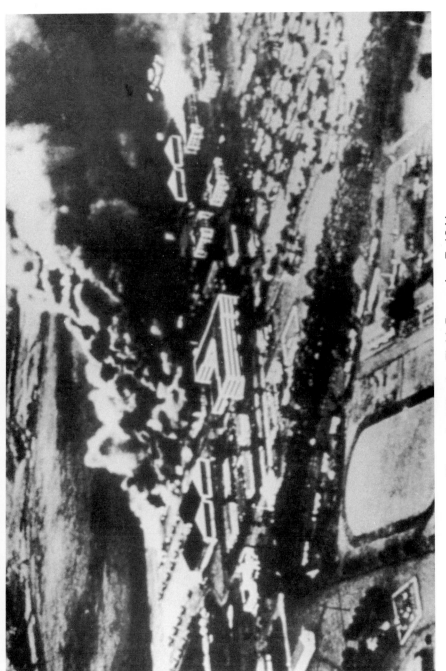

Figure 3. Wheeler Field, December 7, 1941.

Figure 4. Captain Smith (left) making his first inspection of an AAA unit.

Figure 5. Headquarters staff, Hawaiian artillery command.

Figure 6. Hawaiian artillery staff with their guests seated at the banquet table in the Henry Fagin Mansion, Honolulu, Hawaii.

Headquarters Artillery Command
Office of the Commanding General
A. P. O. 958

5 December 1943.

Major William C. Smith,
Building 664,
Camp Davis, N.C.

My dear Smith:

Your first letter arrived some ten days ago and was circulated among the office force. Then, immediately behind that one, came one to Holmes. We were all interested and pleased to hear from you and to learn that you made your way to Camp Davis without too many difficulties.

Yesterday, another note arrived from you inclosing the clippings from the newspaper. I was very much interested in the one showing Colonel Martin receiving his decoration.

I am sorry to note that the school has very little information on the 4.7. It may be that we are taking on a white elephant. However, I have no doubt but that they will be better than the old Navy 5". At the moment we have received one 545 radar. I believe you indicated that you liked the other type better than the 545. Any real dope you can get on this subject will be of great benefit. The periodicals of the country, especially "Time," indicate that we are fully equipped with the finest instruments for firing on unseen targets. I wish this were the case -- perhaps some day we shall be.

This will reach you in time to serve both as a Christmas present and a Christmas greeting. I thank you very much for your kindness in writing; absorb all the real information on antiaircraft you can, and don't forget to come back.

Kindest regards,

H. T. B.

H. T. BURGIN,
Major General, U. S. Army.

P.S.
Last time I saw your date she was in tow of a Vice-Admiral —
HTB

Figure 7. Letter from Major General Henry T. Burgin to Major William Cazy Smith December 5, 1943.

NC111-6/ADCC
Serial 0034

PACIFIC FLEET RADAR CENTER
Navy 91 (Nine One)
c/o Fleet Post Office
San Francisco, Calif.

8 March 1945.

From: Secretary, A.D.C.C. Board.
To: Members, A.D.C.C. Board.
(1) Pacific Fleet Radar Center
(a) Capt. E. M. THOMPSON
(2) Commanding General, U.S. Army Forces, Pacific Ocean Areas.
(a) Col. A. R. MARCY
(b) Lt.Col. R. J. PEISINGER
(c) Lt.Col. W. C. SMITH
(3) Commanding General, U.S. Army Air Forces, Pacific Ocean Areas.
(a) Col. J. M. WEIKERT
(b) Col. R. S. CARTER
(c) Maj. E. F. HETTEL
(4) Commanding General, Fleet Marine Force, U.S. Pacific Fleet.
(a) Col. H. R. PAIGE
(b) Lt.Col. H. H. WILLIAMSON
(c) Maj. G. G. WILLIAMS
(5) Commanding General Aircraft, Fleet Marine Force, U.S. Pacific Fleet.
(a) Lt.Col. H. H. WILLIAMSON
(b) Maj. T. E. HICKS, Jr.
(c) Maj. W. B. MURDOCK
(6) Commander Air Force, U.S. Pacific Fleet.
(a) Lt.Comdr. R. M. FREEMAN
(7) Commander Amphibious Forces, U.S. Pacific Fleet.
(a) Capt. C. F. HORNE
(b) Comdr. H. P. COOPER

Subject: A.D.C.C. Board, Minutes of Third Meeting of.

Enclosures: (A) Minutes of meeting held on 28 February 1945.
(B) Final Draft of Air Defense Doctrine.
(C) Letter from Capt. C. F. HORNE of 15 February 1945 to Senior Member of the A.D.C.C. Board.

1. Enclosure (A) consists of the Minutes of the third meeting of the A.D.C.C. Board. Corrections or revisions should be sent to the secretary.

2. Enclosure (B) is the final draft of the Air Defense Doctrine after incorporation of all changes and modifications made at the Board meeting, and now recommended to CinCPOA.

Figure 8. Membership of Air Defense Control Center Board, Pacific Ocean Areas command.

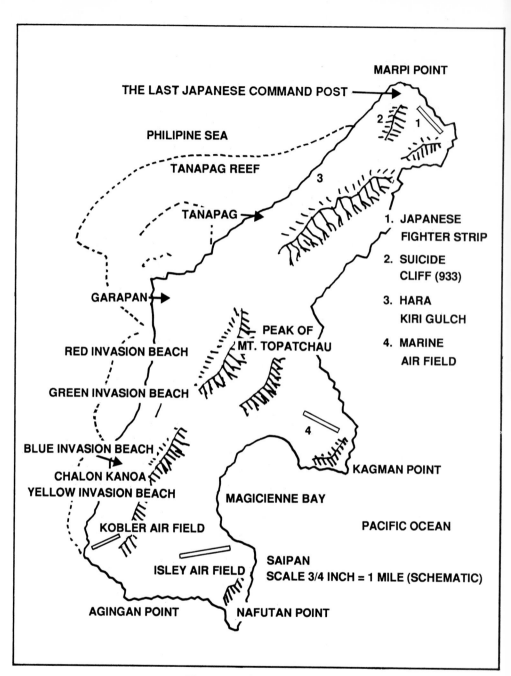

Figure 9. Map of Saipan.

PREPARATION FOR AND MOVEMENT OF TASK FORCE TREE
TO A.P.O. No. 457

ORGANIZATION AND PREPARATION FOR MOVEMENT ---6.1 PHASE   I

MOVEMENT ---2+H-8-------------------------- PHASE II

LANDING OPERATIONS AND FORTIFICATION OF ISLAND --- PHASE III

       The report to follow was based on observations from the artillery-man's point of view which were made with the idea of gaining information that would assist the artillery in planning for such moves in the future. Incidents not directly related to artillery are not given in detail but are mentioned only because of their interest and the part they play to complete the picture.   of

PHASE I

ORGANIZATION AND PREPARATION FOR MOVEMENT

1. Organization:

    a. Artillery units assigned to task force Tree consisted of Anti-aircraft Batteries B, 93d Coast Artillery, (90mm); F, 64th Coast Artillery, (90mm); K and M, 98th Coast Artillery; K and M, 98th Coast Artillery, (37mm and .50 caliber machine guns); and the 3d Platoon of Battery A, 97th Coast Artillery, (S/L). The above batteries were stripped of drivers and motor transportation personnel.

    b. Air Corps troops consisted of the 19th Fighter Group and related aviation service forces.

    c. Engineer troops consisted of the 804th Battalion, Aviation Engineers.

    d. Service troops consisted of detachments from Quartermaster, Chemical, Medical, Ordnance, and Signal Corps.

2. Equipment:

    a. (1) Antiaircraft gun batteries were each equipped with 4 - 90mm guns, 4 - .50 caliber machine guns, 1 - M7 director, 1 - SCR-268 radar, and 1 - M2 stereoscopic height finder.

       (2) Automatic weapons batteries were each equipped with 8 - 37mm guns, 8 - .50 caliber machine guns, and 8 - M5 directors.

       (3) The searchlight platoon was equipped with 6 searchlights, 6 - .50 caliber machine guns, 2 - SCR's-268, and appropriate control equipment.

       (4) Twenty units of fire for all weapons were supplied.

    b. Spare parts and ninety day ordnance supplies were furnished. Inasmuch as no spare parts were available for 37mm guns, one extra gun was supplied.

    c. To give long-range aircraft warning to antiaircraft and Air Corps units, the Signal Corps had for operation one SCR-270 and one SB2C radar.

    d. No transportation was assigned artillery units.

- 1 -

Figures 10-17. Official observer's report on preparation for the movement of Task force tree (Bakers Island, September 20, 1943.)

       e. All guns and fire control instruments were overhauled prior to loading aboard ships. Searchlights and auxilliary equipment were new.

      3. Staging operations:

       a. Artillery units were informed of their assignment 8 August 1943 and instructed to make preparations to move to Bellows Field by 11 August 1943. These preparations included: crating of organizational equipment; delivering armament, except machine guns, to Ordnance; completion of personnel and stock records; and medical inspection. Men with defects or generally undesirable for this duty were transferred out of organizations and replaced by capable men. Units experienced much difficulty in securing appropriate lumber and binding equipment for crating. Inexperience in this type of work contributed to slow progress in crating. All crates were marked with identification symbols.

       b. Movement to Bellows Field was delayed until 15 August 1943. All individual and organizational equipment, plus machine guns, was taken to Bellows Field with personnel. Other Ordnance equipment went directly from Hawaiian Ordnance Depot to the dock area.

       c. Some training was done in the staging area which included two and one-half hours of amphibious training for all troops, firing of the M1 rifle by all troops not having fired before (all artillery troops had previously fired the rifle), and qualification of nonswimmers.

       d. All troops were reexamined by the task force surgeon. As will be shown in log below, this medical inspection took a major portion of the time spent in the staging area.

       e. Log:

      August 15: All units moved to Bellows Field; task force headquarters organized, and amphibious training started.

      August 16: Task force surgeon with assistants initiated medical inspection of personnel. Training program was drawn up and put into force. Shortages in individual and organizational equipment being requisitioned; Bellows Field Quartermaster lending full assistance.

      August 17: Medical inspection continuing. The delay of some regimental units in forwarding medical records interrupted the schedule and caused some confusion. It was disclosed that Batteries K and M, 98th Coast Artillery, had little or no spare parts for automatic weapons; steps were taken to obtain same.

      August 18: One lieutenant rejected by medical inspector. The acceptance of several enlisted men pending on their being able to complete dental repairs.

      August 19: Organizational equipment being loaded as of 0300. Previous indecision as to whether or not machine guns would be crated settled in favor of crating. The engineers at Bellows Field agreed to crate the machine guns, with crates constructed to facilitate guns being removed from crates and placed in firing position on deck of ships. Standard Operating Procedure was drawn up using a copy of Ganton's SOP as a guide. Shortage on transportation slowed down movement of equipment to dock area. Each battery assigned one officer or competent noncommissioned officer as liaison on each ship for observing and advising on loading of equipment.

      August 20: An area similar in size to that to be occupied was staked out on Bellows Field and relative positions assigned to units. An assimilated landing was made from landing craft with representatives from each unit taking up positions on shore in the manner planned for actual landing. Loading of boats completed with exception of machine guns. Medical inspection completed with only a few men eliminated.

(Basic: Preparation for and movement of task force Tree to A.P.O. No. 457.)

August 21: Representatives from Department Headquarters made spot inspection of men for qualifications. "B" bags loaded aboard ship.

August 22: Received report that in loading, 12 rounds of 90mm ammunition had been dropped in water, one 37mm gun damaged enroute to dock, and one M5 director damaged by dropping on dock. The 37mm gun was repaired while the M5 was replaced (this evidently occurred on August 20).

August 23: Guides and kitchen police were taken aboard ship. Inspector General inspected battery records. Inasmuch as these records were crated, this caused confusion and delay. Final preparations made for boarding ships the following day.

PHASE II

MOVEMENT

1. Personnel boarding ship on August 24:

a. Artillery troops were first to board ship. The troops started aboard at 1330 and all were aboard by 1510. Other troops followed with engineer troops the last to come aboard. Loading was completed by 1730.

b. All troops boarded ship with "A" bags and individual equipment. Loading was orderly and on schedule.

c. One man from Battery K, 98th Coast Artillery, was reported AWOL. This man was an alleged conscientious objector. Replacement was accomplished.

2. Composition of naval task force:

a. The task force moved out to sea at 0800 August 25 and was composed of the transport Tyler, freighter Hercules, lighter ship Ashland (LSD-1), 2 aircraft carriers (converted type), and 4 destroyers. The freighter Regulus and 3 corvettes had moved out two days previous.

3. General:

a. Approximately 2,000 troops were aboard the Tyler, while antiaircraft gun crews consisting of 35 men each were aboard the Regulus and Hercules.

b. On the Tyler one mess was operated for troop class passengers and two meals served daily. Servings were arranged by hatches. Permanent kitchen police were assigned and assistant cooks (to ship cooks) drawn from units.

c. Troops were given calisthenics daily on the boat and promenade decks. Continuous police details were maintained throughout daylight hours to keep the ship clean.

d. For security purposes .50 caliber machine guns were set up on deck of ships. Throughout daylight hours, planes from carriers maintained a constant patrol.

e. Many conferences were held by officials and final plans for unloading drawn up.

f. The Regulus joined the convoy at 0730 on August 31. The Regulus being a slow ship the speed of the convoy was reduced from 12 knots to 9 knots.

(Basic: Preparation for and movement of task force Tree to A.P.O. No. 457.)

PHASE III

LANDING OPERATIONS

1. Plan:

a. The original plan for unloading was to have the engineers go ashore first and establish the beach head. With sufficient power equipment ashore to handle unloading and start grading of runway, antiaircraft batteries were to come ashore in order, one gun battery, one automatic weapons battery, one gun battery, one automatic weapons battery, and, finally, searchlights. Simultaneously marston mat was to be unloaded. The long-range radio detectors also held a high priority. As shown in log below, deviations were made.

b. Fourteen landing crafts were preloaded with heavy engineer equipment in the flooding compartments of the LSD-1. This equipment was that scheduled to go ashore first.

2. Log:

September 1: Breakfast was served at 0530 and the island sighted at daylight, 0645. Corvettes proceeded to the leeward side of the island and searched the water area for mines. An armed guard went ashore at 0822 in whale boats, followed by a reconnaissance party at 0830. Liaison officers, unloading details, and winch operators were immediately dispatched to the freighters. At 0915 bulldozer tractors were grading approaches to beach head. The nature of terrain at the beach head was a strip of land from the water's edge, approximately seventy-five feet wide with a sharp incline of twenty feet to the level of the island. Three approaches were graded and paved with sommerfield mat. The sand was very soft but the mat proved very satisfactory. The only trouble experienced with the mat was near the water's edge where tractors had a tendency to tear it up while maneuvering around the landing craft. It was reported that the Ashland had trouble launching her preloaded landing craft. Extremely high waves inside of the flooded compartments had resulted in a craft loaded with a power shovel in the aft compartment overturning. This trapped seven boats in the forward compartment. A maximum of twelve landing craft were observed in operation. By noon three of these were disabled and beached. The heavy swells and choppy water made the task of bringing landing craft along side ships a difficult one. The Navy reported that at 1315 one Japanese four-motored flying boat of the Emily class was shot down by Navy fighters near Howland Island. The plane was disposed of in short order and the probability was that the radio operator did not have time to send a message relative to the encounter. By sundown, approximately one thousand troops were ashore with individual equipment and three days' K rations. These troops consisted mostly of engineers, one battery of antiaircraft troops, quartermaster, and signal corps troops. The first 90mm gun went ashore just before dark. Other troops remained on ship until they were needed on shore. Shortly after dark the Tylor went to sea as a safety precaution. However, landing operations continued from the Hercules. Grading of runway under way on twenty-four hour schedule. The LSD had more trouble. The tail gate was jammed; thus denying employment of normal method of taking on landing craft for servicing. This considerably reduced the number of craft kept in operating condition. Water sterilizer was in operation by early afternoon.

September 2: One complete 90mm battery ashore by 0300. This battery was set up and oriented by daylight. Settling shots were fired shortly thereafter. A total of five landing craft were observed as out of action and beached, two reported as lost at sea during the night. Crews were rescued. Only four landing craft in operation for most of the a.m. Mostly "C" rations being unloaded during the a.m. Three 37mm guns ashore. Shortly after dark an alert was sounded and operations stopped for two hours. The alert was given by ships when lights were suddenly turned off on shore and the report received from beach head of a flare at sea. It was later concluded that

- 4 -

what an observer on shore thought was a flare was actually a shooting star. One SCR-268 in operation and tied in with gun battery for fire control by late afternoon.

September 3: Fearful that enemy action might force ships to put out to sea, beach head officials called for more "C" rations, and most of the day was spent unloading same. Seven boats were observed in operation. Alert sounded at 1320. Radar plot from destroyer indicated several planes were approaching from the northwest. Interception by Navy fighters proved there to be only one. Several passes were required to shoot down the target which was reported as an Emily-type Japanese flying boat. During early afternoon the overturned power shovel was removed from the LSD adding seven more landing craft for operation. A total of sixteen landing craft were observed in operation during the afternoon. Beach facilities had to be expanded to handle the increased number of landing craft.

September 4: Operations were good during the night and for the first time since the landing started the future looked satisfactory. Nine 37mm guns, one M5 director, two SCR's-268, and one SCR-270 ashore and in operation. Grading of runways 3/4 complete. During the afternoon most of the unloading switched to marston mat. One kitchen was set up and "C" ration provided. No favorable reports were heard regarding the "K" ration.

September 5: Mat continued to be unloaded while a large amount of other equipment was also unloaded. Four more 90mm guns ashore but without fire control equipment. More antiaircraft personnel brought ashore; approximately fifty per cent yet aboard Tyler. Portions of the remaining two SCR's -268 ashore.

September 6: Laying of the marston mat was commenced at 1400. All SCR's-268 now ashore and in operation. Total of eleven 37mm guns ready for operation. Two searchlights with equipment and two extra power plants ashore. These two lights were installed with radars and tested. Fire control equipment not yet in for the four 90mm guns brought ashore on the 5th.

September 7: Navy TBF made emergency landing on unpaved portion of landing strip at 1015. The pilot commented favorably on the smoothness of the strip. Navy fighter landed on strip at 1115. The slowness in mat coming off the boat has given graders extra time to improve bed of runway.

September 8: 2,000 feet of mat down. Four searchlights in operation. Mostly mat coming off today. Policy has changed from priority items to "catch as catch can" to mostly mat. One more plane reported shot down at sea with another damaged. Both came in at 1,000 feet and were apparently searching for carriers. By 1800 there was completed 2,500 feet of mat. By late afternoon aviation gas, oil, and miscellaneous Air Corps and antiaircraft equipment began coming ashore. Fire control equipment for second gun battery ashore. Battery made ready for action but height finder was damaged and of no use. Wedges were apparently dislocated. A line was laid to the height finder of Battery B, 93d Coast Artillery, in order to obtain altitudes.

September 9: First plane (PBY5A) came in from Canton with mail. This was also first plane to land on steel mat. Navy planes start using mat regularly. All 37mm guns are ashore except two.

September 10: All guns are ashore except one 37mm gun and six .50 caliber machine guns. These guns are still set up on deck of ships. Made final inspection of antiaircraft guns; all in excellent condition. Only minor damages sustained in unloading. Power plants for 37mm guns all shore. One C-46 and one C-47 came in from Canton. Beef brought in. Organizational equipment coming ashore; also "B" bags. Ships are about three-fourths unloaded. "

September 11: 4,000 feet of mat laid, 5,000 feet of suitable runway available. Eighteen fighters (P-40's) from the 19th Fighter Group landed at 1100. The observer departed from the island for Canton at 1330. On Canton, a height finder was obtained and sent to the task force by air on the morning of September 12.

Comments:

a. In general the landing operation was very satisfactory, but should serious enemy resistance have been encountered, the results would have been doubtful.

b. The rate of unloading was determined by the number of landing craft the Navy was able to keep in operation. On the average, approximately five landing craft were kept in operation. Ships did not anchor but drifted for discharging cargo. However, a two knot current continually swept the ships out to sea. After drifting out about four miles, ships would cease operations and return to a point approximately one-fourth mile offshore.

c. The task force was well protected by a constant air patrol; carrier based planes by day and night fighters from Canton by night.

d. Morale was excellent at all times. However, when operations fell far behind schedule there was a tendency for some officers to become disgruntled and relax their efforts.

e. Artillery and engineer troops were outstanding in their ability to adjust themselves to field conditions. However, many rules of field sanitation were not observed.

f. Debarkation was virtually on the open sea and so hazardous as to have very little resemblance to conditions imposed in amphibious training on Oahu. Despite this hazard no casualties occurred to task force troops. Two Navy men had both legs broken and one man suffered a broken hand. These accidents were caused by landing craft being thrown against the side of ship by waves. While debarking all men wore life jackets.

g. Frequently the motors on landing craft would quit while between ship and shore allowing the craft to drift out to sea. One craft was rescued at a distance of 54 miles from the island.

h. It was noted that when guns came ashore usually the regular crews were not present to man the equipment and crews had to be made up consisting of cooks, power plant operators, etc. It was disappointing to find that many of these men were untrained to perform such duties.

i. Instances were noted where battery commanders were slow in organizing gun crews with the men and equipment available, and assumptions were made that certain automatic weapons were ready for action while a close inspection revealed the opposite. Also it was noted that on several occasions where conditions prevented normal procedure the second best solution was not attempted. As an example of misdirected efforts one battery commander of a 90mm battery was expending great effort to obtain lumber for constructing bunkers, meanwhile neglecting to improvise a means for obtaining altitudes (a simple task).

j. In this operation construction of the landing mat held high priority, with the priority of antiaircraft armament fluctuating with the gravity of the situation. However, there appeared to be a false sense of security by officials in charge during various phases of the operation in that the defensive value of guns without fire control equipment and searchlights was overrated.

k. Early in landing operations the Engineer Battalion took its own .50 caliber machine guns ashore for defense against enemy aircraft while the guns of antiaircraft batteries remained on the boat. By virtue

- 8 -

of training, the antiaircraft would have been more suited for performing this mission. Also, in that engineer equipment was later to be reloaded, lost effort and valuable cargo space was taken up by the movement of these guns.

l. Ship to shore contact was maintained by radio. The greatest hazard encountered at the beach head was keeping the landing craft headed into the beach for unloading. This problem was solved by employing tractors and amphibious tanks to hold the craft straight into shore. Most useful in unloading cargo from landing craft was the "Cherry Picker." On the beach tractors and power cranes were very useful. For hauling cargo from beach head, dump trucks proved very useful. The amphibious truck proved to be a good utility machine. It was able to maneuver in the water or on the sandy beach with ease.

m. Equipment that was well crated came ashore in far better condition than that crated without expert assistance. Some poorly constructed crates burst open allowing articles to drop out and become lost.

4. Recommendations:

a. For all future movements of this nature, crating of all equipment be accomplished by, or under the supervision, of expert personnel.

b. Staging operations be held near the dock area to permit more active participation in loading of ships by officers of the task force.

c. (1) Emphasis be placed on qualifying antiaircraft personnel to perform many duties within the battery.

(2) Field sanitation receive more emphasis.

(3) Officers and noncommissioned officers be impressed with their responsibility in maintaining an organized fighting unit under all conditions.

d. Irregularities noted above, not related to functions of the artillery, be brought to the attention of the appropriate service.

WM. C. SMITH,
Major, C.A.C.

370.09   1st Ind.   HTB/ilr

HEADQUARTERS ARTILLERY COMMAND, A.P.O. No. 958 - 20 September 1943.

TO: Commanding General, Seacoast Artillery Command, A.P.O. No. 956.
Commanding General, Antiaircraft Artillery Command, A.P.O. No. 958.

1. The report of the operations of the task force for "Tree" is furnished you for information, remark, and recommendation.

2. Especial emphasis is directed to the following outstanding features of the report:

a. Failure of operation of landing barges. Regardless of how well planned the ship to shore movement may be, it is inevitable that something will occur to disrupt these plans. It is essential that there be an alternate plan to meet every contingency. The failure of landing craft to function as planned reduced the number of craft available far below expectations and the sequence of movement was thrown entirely out of gear. Pro-

loading of equipment and assignment of personnel for ship to shore movement should be planned to meet such contingencies.

     b. Handling of delicate instruments. It is imperative that all delicate instruments, directors, height finders, etc., which are subject to serious injury due to normal loading methods, be preloaded in landing craft. The destruction, loss, or damage of such instruments precludes efficient operation of armament and every precaution should be taken to insure safe delivery. Initial packing and crating should be accomplished by experienced personnel.

     c. Training of personnel. Training directives and policies have always expressed the necessity of individuals being able to perform all duties within the firing unit. The lack of such training was noted in some of the units comprising this task force. Any gun without operating personnel is useless and the availability of personnel sufficiently trained to place a gun in immediate action is essential. Unit commanders should, during landing operations, keep a constant check on grouping of personnel to afford maximum efficiency of operation of the weapons as they go ashore.

     d. Attitude of commissioned officers. The quality of leadership of officers and noncommissioned officers is demonstrated by their ability to function when "the going gets tough." As stated before, operation will seldom, if ever, go according to plans. Officers must be able to provide expedients with a minimum of delay. The harder the problem, the more active an officer must become to obtain an immediate solution. "Crying over spilt milk" and damning the causes for the failure of any plan, will accomplish nothing except "loss of face" in the eyes of subordinates. Prompt, decisive action to remedy the situation will, on the other hand, develop a sense of trust and the knowledge that the officer is a capable leader.

    3. Full use will be made of the information contained in the attached report in the preparation and training of future task forces.

H. T. BURGIN,
Major General, U. S. Army,
Commanding.

- 8 -

ARTILLERY OFFICE
CENTRAL PACIFIC AREA
A.P.O. No. 958

Auth: Artillery Officer
Initials: [illegible] Executive Officer
Date: 7/7/44

5 July 1944.

SUBJECT: Observer's Report.

TO: Commanding General, U.S. Army Forces, Central Pacific Area.

1. Reference is made to the following:

   a. Paragraph 1, letter orders, Headquarters, Central Pacific Area, dated 6 May 1944.

   b. Fourth Indorsement to letter orders, Headquarters, Central Pacific Area, dated 8 May 1944.

2. In compliance with references in the observer reported to the Commanding General, Fifth Amphibious Corps, for the purpose of acting as an observer in operations against the Marianas Islands. Subsequently by reference 1b the observer was directed to report to the Commanding officer of the antiaircraft unit participating in the assault on Saipan, for temporary duty thereunder. The observer departed from Saipan on 30 June 1944.

3. Organization:

   a. For the purpose of providing antiaircraft protection to troops and equipment in the assault on Saipan, antiaircraft units were withdrawn from Army Garrison forces ... 244 and assigned this mission. In order to obtain maximum antiaircraft protection with the personnel involved, all units selected for the assault were stripped to the minimum of personnel consistent with immediate requirements for efficient operation. The units involved were:

UNIT	D	O	E
1. Hq 98th AAA Group.	5	-	15
2. Hq 94th AAA Autogps Bn.	5	-	6
3. Btrys A, B, C, & D, 864th Auto Wpn Bn.	16	-	342
4. Btrys A & B, 751st AAA Gun Bn.	10	-	160
5. Provisional AAA Gun Group Staff	2	1	2

In addition to the above strength, one medical aid man was attached to each battery, and two medical officers were attached to the group.

052/42 - Observer's Report.
5 July 1944 - cont'd.

   b. One gun battery and two automatic weapons batteries, with personnel, were combat loaded on each of two LST's. All battalion and group headquarters personnel, except the 98th AAA Group, were divided equally and placed aboard the two LST's for transportation. The antiaircraft commander, with his executive officer, the observer, and twelve enlisted men of the 98th AAA Group were assigned transportation on the Command ship for Northern Troops and Landing forces. This was for the purpose of close liaison with the Commanding General, Northern Troops and Landing Force, and utilizing ship's information on enemy aircraft. The plan was to transmit, by use of the CR-300, plots of enemy aircraft to shore-based antiaircraft in the initial phase until radars could be installed. Actually, this service was never used because the CR-602 radars were in operation on shore by the time antiaircraft units were ready for action.

   c. (1) Because of the limited capacity of the LST, each automatic weapons battery was reduced to seven sections. All of the 40mm guns were emplaced for action on the top decks of the LST's.

     (2) In addition to normal armament, one multiple gun motor carriage M16 was assigned to each of the automatic weapons batteries. This piece of equipment proved valuable on this operation. It came ashore through three to four feet of water with ease and was used on shore for many things to include, reconnaissance, hauling water and rations, and as a prime mover for 40mm guns. Its light armor was a comfort to the operators in areas inhabited by snipers.

     (3) Antiaircraft gun batteries had VHF equipment of guns and fire control equipment. Each battery was equipped with an M-9 director and fire control radar CR-545.

     (4) None of the assault did not contain ordnance personnel or a meteorological section.

4. The Assault:

   a. Antiaircraft units were prepared to land on call on D day. At H plus four hours, the Commanding General, Northern Troops and Landing Forces, ordered LST's with antiaircraft equipment to line of departure and instructed the beachmaster to make a reconnaissance of the beaches in company with the antiaircraft commander to determine where and if antiaircraft could be landed. The reconnaissance party returned from the beach and reported that the beachmaster had desired it unsafe to beach LST's because of heavy enemy artillery fire on the reef and beaches. Very little chance in security of the beachhead was noted on D plus One, and unloading of antiaircraft equipment was again delayed.

Figures 18-26. Official observer's report of the Saipan operation By Lt. Col. William Cazy Smith, dated 7 July, 1944.

and battalion commanders, landed and prepared to receive all the antiaircraft units. In the meantime, an effort was being made to transship antiaircraft equipment to beaches in LCM's. Unloading operations continued until darkness. During the day two 90mm guns, one .4 tractor, four multiple motor carriages M-16, and fire control equipment for one gun battery were landed. The one director unloaded was drowned out and consequently rendered of no value to the battery. The ramp on one LST was damaged while transferring equipment to an LCM.

c. The method of transshipping on LCM' was abandoned on D plus Three in favor of beaching LST on the reef at a point where there was no lagoon. The equipment was to be landed on the reef at low tide when depth of water was about eighteen inches. Difficulties occurred in that the slope of the reef was too gradual, and the ramp of the LST could not extend to shallow water. The final and successful method was obtained by placing a pontoon causeway on the reef and approaching the causeway with LCT's. The causeway was maneuvered into position at the reef by use of LCT's and LVT's then pulled onto the reef by use of two D-8 tractors. Antiaircraft equipment was unloaded the following day (D plus Four) without incident. The performance of the .4 tractors in three to four feet of water as well as on land was outstanding.

d. The first echelon of antiaircraft garrison troops was scheduled for D plus Three but did not arrive until D plus Twelve. This force contained the remaining personnel of a squad units, the 501st AAA Gun Battalion, and Battery B, 296th Searchlight Battalion. The personnel of the 501st AAA Gun Battalion were dispatched immediately to their selected battery areas to prepare for receipt of equipment. The following day this equipment started arriving on the various beaches in driblets, but no battery was completely equipped until D plus Fourteen (29 June). At this time a spare SCR director was received to replace the one drowned out on D plus Two. Although instructions were received from the beach party to the effect that this equipment would land on a particular beach, actually it came in on all beaches. To intercept this equipment it was necessary to patrol constantly all beaches in search for equipment.

5. Organization and operation of shore.

a. (1) Initially the available beach area suitable for emplacing antiaircraft gun batteries at a reasonably safe distance from enemy small fire was restricted. Consequently, in order to obtain the best tactical disposition of guns, it was necessary to move soil for the first few days in a gradual approach to permanent positions. Each gun battery borrowed two bulldozers from the Army garrison force engineer. These were of inestimable value to the batteries in clearing the way for and assisting in erecting good gun emplacements. When

---

bags were used to line bunkers. The bunkers were completed by backfilling with dirt.

(2) The two 90mm gun batteries (one without director) were employed to render maximum protection to Aslito Airfield and the southern portion of the beachhead.

(3) Three 40mm batteries were set up in defense of the beachhead.

(4) One 40mm battery defended Aslito Airfield.

b.

(1) Assault antiaircraft units went into action for the first time at 1845 on D plus Two. The 40mm guns on deck of LST's and the four .50-16's ashore went into action against two low-flying single engine planes. Many were o.s of all calibers belonging to units under maximum antiaircraft fire firing, and credit for downing one of the two planes could not be established, but observers in the vicinity of one of the .50-16's say that this weapon was responsible for downing the aircraft.

(2) During the night of D plus Two, five separate flights of enemy aircraft came over the island. Four of these flights were fired on by the one antiaircraft gun battery in operation. On each occasion the aircraft turned and went out after the first burst. The destruction of one enemy aircraft was later confirmed. "Hold fire" was given by the antiaircraft commander because of the presence of a friendly plane in the area, and during this interim one enemy aircraft dropped bombs near Charon Kanoa.

(3) Two enemy aircraft came over the area at about 1950 on D plus Ten. The first plane dropped four bombs on the billeting area of Aslito Airfield. The second aircraft dropped flares over the transport area. The antiaircraft gun battery was in "hold fire," but tracked the aircraft with good data. Fleet antiaircraft guns were in action.

(4) Enemy aircraft were over the island intermittently from 1900, 27 June, to 0030, 28 June. A total of five flights came within range of the antiaircraft guns, and all flights were fired on. Bombs were dropped on four of the five runs, but planes were under fire at the time and bombs hit no worthy target. Two enemy aircraft were

listed as probably destroyed. Altitude of planes varied from 14,000 to 30,000 feet.

(6) At 2016 on 28 June one enemy aircraft dropped bombs near Aslito Airfield. Guns were in "hold fire" because of the presence of an artillery liaison plane in the vicinity. Guns were released to fire and did so after bombs had been dropped. The results were unknown. At 2035 one enemy aircraft approached Aslito Airfield and was destroyed by antiaircraft gunfire. The plane caught on fire and exploded before reaching the ground. This action was very dramatic and was cheered loudly by all the troops. An infantry battalion commander reported the following day that this particular action was the biggest morale booster his troops had experienced since landing on the island. An enemy aircraft came in on a run for Aslito Airfield. The aircraft was taken under fire by antiaircraft guns and destroyed.

c. In a secondary role, antiaircraft units delivered terrestrial fire in support of infantry units.

(1) On 21 June, 90mm antiaircraft gunfire was delivered on ground targets in the area north of Magicienne Bay. Fighty rounds were expended on five assigned targets, but unfavorable observation rendered the value of this fire as doubtful.

(2) Counterbattery fire was placed on Tinian by antiaircraft guns on 22 June. Again poor observation denied good adjustment, and the results were doubtful.

(3) On 25, 26, and 27 June, a total of 1,300 rounds of 90mm ammunition were expended on point targets in support of infantry units on Nafutan Point. The terrain was extremely rugged, and fire delivered by field artillery and heavy mortars had not produced the desired effects. However, air bursts were able to reach crevices and depths of rocky surfaces to obtain good results. Simultaneously 40mm guns were employed about one thousand yards from the target area and fired into caves with complete success. The infantry battalion commander was highly pleased and enthusiastic over the fire delivered by antiaircraft units and expressed the opinion that much time and many personnel were saved by this support. This officer gave credit to the antiaircraft for killing between two hundred and three hundred of approximately

eight hundred enemy dead found in the area. Of particular interest was the fact that fire from the 90mm guns was more accurate when delivered by field artillery methods without use of the director. Original data were obtained from a map. For this type of firing guns must be oriented with true north, and the battery commander should set accordingly in anticipation of this type of firing.

d. The plan for control of shore-based antiaircraft was that the fleet air assault officer would, from aboard the control ship, announce through the Commanding General, Northern Troop and Landing Force, the condition of alert and the control of fire. Inasmuch as the antiaircraft commander received no condition of fire through 22 June, the failure of the plan needs no further evidence or comment. This condition existed in spite of repeated pleas by the antiaircraft commander for this information. In desperation the antiaircraft commander announced his own condition through radar identification of aircraft. Occasionally word reached the antiaircraft commander that friendly aircraft were in the area. On one occasion fire was held on enemy aircraft because of information that friendly aircraft were in the area. It was later discovered that friendly aircraft were not within gun range at the moment.

e. All firing at aircraft by shore-based antiaircraft guns was unseen and controlled by the radar SCR-545. It was found that firing with the radar in automatic control produced better results than manual tracking. Momentary illumination of the target by burst revealed that in manual tracking the burst had a tendency to trail the target slightly.

f. The search mission performed by the radars SCR's 602 were of much value. The Army 726th and Marine 5th Air Warning Companies manned these radars and gave information on all targets. Although many targets approached the island simultaneously, the information from the search radars made it possible on each occasion for the guns to pick up and track the appropriate target.

g. The enemy consistently dropped "window", but inasmuch as the SCR-545 tracked through it without difficulty, the effect was nil.

h. Each headquarters, down to include section, was equipped with the SCR-300 set for the assault. This radio was a "lifesaver" and was extremely satisfactory. One hazard encountered was the fact that some field artillery units had the same set and frequency. Occasionally this slowed down transmission. The shortage of experienced operators was in evidence. The only mechanical or electrical trouble was experienced by a few sets failing to transmit. This failure was traced to a rusty diaphragm sticking to the poles of the electromagnet. As the units received and set up, the C's 543 and 583, the C's 300 were gradually withdrawn. Although field wire was laid between units, this type of communication could not be maintained. The greatest care in laying wire could not prevent it from being cut or broken.

i. To the average antiaircraft officer the subject of local security has been rather theoretical and of secondary importance. To the antiaircraft personnel in this operation it became real and paramount. Examples of action included:

    (1) Repelling enemy infiltration.

    (2) Digging enemy snipers out of position.

    (3) Capturing enemy soldiers.

    (4) Capturing civilian personnel.

6. Conclusions:

a. The reduced strength for antiaircraft units in the assault presented no serious problems to normal operation. However, ordnance maintenance personnel and a meteorological section should have been included in the assault units. The organic weapons of units other than antiaircraft provide a fair defense against low-flying planes. For the total number of antiaircraft personnel involved, it is believed that in this operation an increase in the number of gun batteries and a decrease in the number of automatic weapons batteries would have been more suitable for the mission.

b. The M-4 tractor and the multiple gun motor carriage M-16 performed well and were very valuable to the units. The bulldozer should be listed as a "must" item for antiaircraft guns in the assault.

c. The Navy personnel responsible for unloading antiaircraft technical equipment were not familiar with this equipment and tended to think only in terms of guns in planning for unloading.

d. Regardless of water-proofing, antiaircraft technical equipment must not be unloaded and pulled through water more than eighteen inches in depth.

e. Two days were lost in getting antiaircraft gun battery ashore, and one director was dropped out because of costly experimentation on how to unload this equipment.

f. The one antiaircraft gun battery which was in order for action performed its mission without fault and vindicated its inclusion

in the assault force.

g. Neither large area ground targets nor unseen point targets are suitable targets for antiaircraft 90mm guns, but observed point or small area targets are suitable, and in the case of rugged terrain, the air burst may be preferred over the normal ground burst. The use of firing tables for preparation of data was found more suitable than use of the director for this type of firing.

h. The plan for control of antiaircraft fire for shore-based guns met with complete failure.

i. "Window" had very little effect on the ability to track aircraft with the SCR-546. The superior performance of the radar SCR-545 results in a question as to the need of searchlights with guns for purposes other than intelligence.

j. The SCR-300 was most valuable to units for communication.

k. The subject of local security became a reality to antiaircraft personnel participating in this operation.

7. Recommendations: It is recommended that;

a. For future operations, where antiaircraft units are involved in the assault, a meteorological section and selected ordnance maintenance personnel be included.

b. Thirty-two multiple gun motor carriages M-16 be requisitioned and made available for assignment to automatic weapons battalions which are to participate in an assault. These weapons should be in lieu of, but later replaced by normal .50 caliber armament of the unit.

c. One bulldozer, with operator, be temporarily assigned to each antiaircraft gun battery which is to participate in an assault. This equipment may be borrowed, with operator, from an engineer unit of the garrison force.

d. Experiments be conducted and a definite decision and understanding between Army and Navy be reached on how antiaircraft equipment should be landed on various types of beaches.

e. Prior to any operation the antiaircraft commander discuss the control of antiaircraft fire with the Navy officer responsible.

052/42 - Observer's Report.
5 July 1944 - cont'd.

insure that the two officers understand each other, and that air intelligence will reach the antiaircraft commander on shore in definite terms.

. Antiaircraft units be given more field problems with conditions imposed to simulate combat conditions.

WM. C. SMITH,
Lt. Col., C.A.C.,
AA Arty. Section.

Figure 27. Aerial photo (June 15, 1944) of Saipan assault.

Figure 28. First wave action on the landing beaches of Saipan June 15, 1944.

Figure 29. Tank now on Perilous Reef is first to hit the beach.

Figure 30. Under enemy fire.

Figure 31. Tank shields marines as they cautiously move forward.

Figure 32. Action on Red Beach.

Figure 33. Saipan, June 1944. Marine throws grenade at Japanese holed up in cave.

Figure 34. Marine hurling grenade in attack on Japanese strong point.

Figure 35. Marine guarding bodies of slain comrades in arms.

Figure 36. Garapan, Saipan under siege June, 1944.

Figure 37. Saipan, June, 1944. Aftermath of Japanese counter thrust in marsh area between Chalon Kanoa and high ground.

• The POA Defense •

The most prominent celebrities I recall are Judy Garland and James Cagney. Cagney passed the camp in his rattletrap Ford many times on his way to work. Because movie stars were held in such awe at this time it was a revelation to learn that they were just ordinary, warmhearted people when they were away from the cameras.

This was a time when many men were in need of work, and the Civilian Conservation Corps helped to relieve the unemployment situation by hiring a dozen or so local specialists at each camp. These were older men who had knowledge of the area and were usually experienced woodsmen. Since few of these men were educated, and some could neither read nor write, they were also given the opportunity to participate in our classes. In addition to this they were paid wages comparable to local rates. Regular members were paid thirty dollars per month, of which twenty-five dollars was sent home to their families.

Some of the most impoverished young men, who had never eaten the quality or quantity of food the Corps provided for them, were anxious to volunteer for kitchen duty. But after gorging themselves for a few weeks they usually expressed their desire to transfer to a regular project detail. Some of the younger, homesick men wanted to be discharged after only a month of this duty but would reconsider when reminded of the shortage of jobs. I recall when a very personable young man received his first monthly wages came to me and asked to be discharged. The reason he gave me was that he had never had any money in his life before, and he wanted to go home and spend it. I told him that his excuse was not a valid reason for discharge and also to think of the amount of money he would have to take home at the end of his service. When he thought about the advantages of staying he was happy to go back to work.

My service in the Civilian Conservation Corps rewarded me in many ways, but the most important was the financial help I received. Because of my salary I was able to join forces with my sister Beatrice—who was Executive Secretary to Tennessee U.S. Senator, George L. Barry in Washington D.C.—to send two younger brothers, Wade and Russell, through four years of schooling at the University of Tennessee in Knoxville.

2

WAR ON THE HORIZON

In late November of 1940, I received a letter from the War Department asking that I accept a call to enter extended active duty with the U.S. Army. Since a national emergency had not been declared, I did not have to accept, but for some time I had anticipated this action and had planned to accept. In fact, I had reentered the Civilian Conservation Corps in preparation of this action by the War Department and was stationed at a camp in Griffith Park, Los Angeles, California when the letter came. I was immediately ordered first to Fort Ord, California, for a physical examination, then to Fort Monroe, Virginia.

My reporting date was December 7, 1940, which allowed four days to travel three thousand miles. I had a 1939 model Chevrolet and decided to drive East on the infamous Route 66. I spent the second night of my long trip at my parents' home in Memphis, Tennessee. While I was in college they had moved to Whitehaven, a suburb of Memphis, to start a retail dairy business. Our visit was much too short, and after an emotional good-bye the next morning I was back on the road for the last leg of my trip to Fort Monroe.

Fort Monroe is located at Old Point Comfort overlooking Hampton Roads, Virginia. It was headquarters for the coast defenses of Chesapeake Bay and site of the Coast Artillery School. I was assigned to the school with a group of two hundred other Reserve Officers for a four months refresher course in Army Antiaircraft Artillery (AAA). This group was comprised of Captains selected from the various other states.

Several young officers from Central and South America had joined us in our studies. Their wives had accompanied them, and they all appeared to be from very wealthy families. These young officers and their wives were the life of the party at the Saturday night dances held at the Officers Club. "Why do they quit?" one of the wives used to exclaim when the band signaled the end of the party, "when we just get started."

The Officers Club occupied the old moat which in Civil War days was a part of the Fortress Monroe. Air Force officers from nearby Langley Field and the Naval officers from Hampton Roads were also a part of the exotic and cosmopolitan group attending the dances. The variety of personnel and the historic atmosphere gave us some exciting evenings.

When our studies were completed we were transferred along with other career senior officers to Camp Davis, North Carolina. We were to staff the AAA units which were to be activated as soon as facilities at the camp were completed. We used public office buildings in Wilmington to organize and prepare for new inductees.

The great reception we received from the people of Wilmington made a lasting impression on me. Leading citizens of the city welcomed the opportunity to take us into their homes until our quarters were completed at Camp Davis. We felt like VIPs when these people opened not only their homes but also their hearts to us. Captain Henry Conners and I lived with Mr. and Mrs. Harry Solomon and their three lovely young daughters, Maria, Jean, and Catherine. The Solomons were leading citizens in Wilmington and went to great lengths to make us feel like a part of their family. We were invited to Sunday morning pancake breakfasts and enjoyed the privileges of the country club.

Then in June 1941, the Army asked for volunteers to be transferred to the Hawaiian department to staff new AAA regiments being organized there. By this time it appeared that our involvement in World War II was imminent so I decided to volunteer. My decision was influenced by a desire to cooperate with officials in their effort to strengthen our armed forces in the Pacific, and besides, the geography of the Pacific area had always appealed to me.

My move to Hawaii was not without deeply emotional and heart-searching moments. My thoughts went back to the movies I had seen about World War I, where young men waved from troop trains and massed on the decks of troop ships to wave a last good-bye as they sailed off to do battle. Many never returned. The script of my movement to Hawaii seemed to follow this pattern completely.

I drove to Fort Eustis near Newport News, Virginia from Camp Davis and arrived the evening before I was to board a troop train bound for San Francisco and the Port of Embarcation.

Many of the townspeople gathered with the band at the train to wish us "bon voyage" on the morning of our departure from Fort Eustis, July 8, 1941. When the train pulled away from the station I watched these wonderful people as long as I could, wondering if I would ever see any of them again.

I had many hours for thought during the next four days as I viewed the countryside from the train windows. Even though I had made cross country rides before while in the Civilian Conservation Corps, this time was different, and my thoughts were more profound. I felt a need to find some diversion from my thoughts and spending time with the conductors served this purpose.

Railroad conductors had always impressed me as being in a unique category all their own. I enjoyed chatting with them and found myself looking forward to the routine change of conductors. Our conductor for the first day out of Virginia was one of the most interesting. He was very personable and had ridden this route for so many years he seemed to recognize many of the people along the way. In fact, I was beginning to believe the old wives tale about the amorous train men when he frequently broke off our conversations to go to the door to wave at someone he knew along the way. When I kidded him about it he just gave me an infectious grin and peered at me over his glasses. As we traveled along through Indiana, I asked him to point out our location on a map I had brought along. After a few glances at the map and the countryside, he appeared to be confused and unable to match them. He replied with the driest of wit, "We're lost."

I was anxious to make a telephone call to my home in Memphis at some point along the route and, after being assured by the conductor that I would have plenty of time, I made the call from Kansas City, Missouri. There had been little time prior to my transfer to tell my mother, father, or the rest of my family about this move. I tried to crowd a lifetime into the few minutes I had on the phone and must have just rattled aimlessly because I cannot remember any of it. When I re-boarded the train and took my seat, I stared out the window and tried hard not to be homesick. On that rainy, dreary day traveling across Kansas I sat with my head pressed against the damp glass and allowed my thoughts to overtake me. I remember I learned something about cows, horses, and sheep that gloomy day. Although I had lived on a farm most of my life, I had never before noticed that in rainy, windy weather a horse stands with his head away from the direction of the wind, a cow wanders aimlessly in all directions, and sheep huddle close together.

On the third morning we arrived in Tucumcari, New Mexico. The kitchen force had advised me that we needed ice and that we were low on kerosene for our cooking stoves. I talked to the conductor, and he assured me we would have forty-five minutes in Tucumcari to replenish these items. I assigned a crew for this duty, and while I waited for them to return I went into the railroad station restaurant for a good breakfast. I had finished my bacon and eggs and was enjoying a second cup of coffee when I noticed that our train was beginning to move. At first I thought they were just making a slight adjustment in their position, and went back to my coffee. But when I glanced up again I realized the train was gaining speed, and I rushed out to get aboard. Too late, I foolishly stood on the tracks waving my arms while the train faded in the distance. Moments later the kitchen crew returned with their supplies, and we stood there together staring down the empty track.

I was very agitated as it had only been twenty minutes since we had left the train. It didn't help my mood any to have the supervisor of a railroad work crew walk up to me and smugly say, "Guess that will teach you to stay on the train." I got my revenge though when our conductor noticed his error and had the train back up for us. When we saw the train returning I casually replied, "Guess that will teach them not to run off and leave us."

In Los Angeles we again had problems. The retiring conductor told us we would have a one hour wait at the station, and we decided to use this time to allow the troops to get off for exercise. This time I got off but walked up and down alongside the train. After about thirty minutes the train began to move slowly forward. I jumped back on board but by the time I could move through the cars to where the conductor was we had moved a great distance. The conductor had no other choice but to stop the train and return, which he did with great anger and disgust. Among those we had left behind was our Army doctor. He and three or four other officers had located a bar close by the station and came aboard "feeling no pain" as the saying goes. It didn't take the good doctor long to soothe our new conductor and have him laughing along with the merrymakers.

We finally arrived in San Francisco and proceeded to the dock area of the Presidio where we transferred to our ship, the *President Coolidge*. This was to be my first ocean voyage, and I was awed by all the luxury. The *President Coolidge* was a luxury liner leased to the United States Maritime Service. It had catered to the affluent who cruised the Pacific area in more peaceful times. The

• An Eyewitness Account •

Maritime Service retained its original staff, and they continued the superior standard of service and quality of food. The only thing missing was its former entertainers.

It was mid-morning and we were to sail by mid-afternoon. By the time they announced "all ashore that's going ashore," excitement had reached a high pitch on deck as friends and loved ones exchanged parting good-byes. There was no one to see me off so I tried desperately to get the attention of someone, anyone, on the dock to whom I could exchange a farewell, but it was all in vain. I remained on deck until we were some distance off shore not only to get a long, last look at the fading mainland, but also because I was fascinated by all the maneuvers necessary to get us underway.

This was July 14, 1941, yet I suddenly realized as we moved to the open sea that I was about as chilled as I had ever been. Little did I suspect the Japanese were already working on plans to strike Pearl Harbor, and that in less than five months I would be the person closest to, and looking directly at, the oncoming plane which fired the first shot of World War II.

After surviving that first rough night at sea, the voyage was made more pleasant and rewarding, largely because of the presence of the United States Ambassador to China who was aboard. I enjoyed his company very much. He was an extravert who had no trouble finding good listeners for his rhetoric.

Captain Dismukes, a former classmate at Mississippi State University, was also aboard. He was with a large group of military personnel destined for the Philippine Islands. I never saw him again, but I later learned that he survived the infamous Bataan Death March. Prior to the end of the war some of our comrades were rescued, and I saw a few of these men as they passed through Hawaii on their way home. Their appearance was shocking: I was stunned by their emaciated state.

On the fifth morning out, I went on deck early to glimpse the first view of the islands. The first thing to come in sight on the horizon was the almost constant cloud coverage over the mountains of Oahu Island. The clouds appeared to be hovering motionless above the mountains, yet as we drew closer it became obvious they were moving. They formed instantly on the windward (northeast) side and evaporated as they passed over the mountains. By the time we reached the vicinity of Diamond Head, we had slowed to a crawl and were no longer jarred by the noise of the ship's engines. This was a beautiful, gentle way to move around the island and into Honolulu Harbor. Our arrival was made even more welcome by an Army band on the dock playing "Aloha Oi." We had truly arrived! Buses were standing by to take us to Schofield Barracks where I learned my assignment was Battery Commander, Battery C, 98th Antiaircraft Artillery.

It was Sunday morning, July 18, 1941. The weather was beautiful, with the sun already bright and warm. Several of my peers were wearing shorts and lay about basking in the sun near my assigned barracks. The voice of Helen O'Connell rang from a portable radio with her recent hit tune, "Green Eyes." I knew I was going to like it here.

The enlisted personnel assigned to my unit at Schofield barracks consisted of a cadre of regular troops and two hundred new recruits with three months basic training. The antiaircraft battery was equipped with four three-inch antiaircraft guns and four fifty-caliber machine guns. Our objective was to train our personnel in the operation of equipment and firearms, including use of the bayonet, and instruction in military defense tactics. They were also trained in health care, sanitation, and how to cope with the hazards of warfare.

My duties at Schofield barracks soon became routine. Although we maintained a full schedule of training, we also had ample free time for sports and social activity. The Officers Club was the main gathering place for social activities, and formal attire was mandatory. Hawaiian evenings, good music, white formal jackets, and beautiful ladies were invigorating for the ego. Pomp and show were at their best in Hawaiian military circles where the theme was "work hard and play hard." On Saturday nights, we usually visited the more elaborate Officers Clubs at Pearl Harbor and Fort Shafter or the Over The Surf pavilion at Fort DeRussy which was adjacent to Waikiki Beach. Because in these circumstances there were few unattached ladies who might require our attention, my fellow officers and I spent a lot of time at the bar and slot machines.

On December 6, 1941, I attended the Hula Bowl in Honolulu, with a group of fellow officers. This was my first experience with a large gathering of local people in Hawaii. The bright colors worn by the fans, the grass-skirted cheerleaders, the Hawaiian music and the exotic air were all enchanting, and I was soon caught up in the magic of the islands. After the game I remember that we went to the Royal Hawaiian Hotel for cocktails. At this time the Royal Hawaiian had been taken over by the Navy and was alive with military personnel. From there we went to the club at Fort Shafter for dinner and dancing. The evening gave no hint of foreboding. In fact, at our command level we had no knowledge officially or unofficially of a threat to our security.

3

DAY OF INFAMY

December 7, 1941, was not unlike many other Sunday morn-
ings I had enjoyed since being sent to Hawaii. I remember I was
lying in bed reading the morning paper, feeling very much at
peace when suddenly I was startled by the noise of numerous
planes approaching from the direction of Kole Kole Pass, just
west of my quarters. As a part of our training, we had learned to
identify all our own American planes by the sound of their
motors, and I knew instantly that these planes were not ours. My
first thought was that they must be German.

I ran outside for a closer look and, when the first planes
swooped down the Rising Sun emblem was plainly visible. At
that instant the lead aircraft fired the first shot of the war in the
Pacific area. The Zero was so close, I could have hit it with a rock.
I learned later that the short volley fired from the lead plane was
the way the lead pilot pointed out the target to his wing men. In
this case their targets were the fighter planes and facilities at
Wheeler Field adjacent to the south side of Schofield Barracks
and about one-third of a mile from my location. The time was
7:50 a.m. and was only minutes before other planes attacked Pearl
Harbor.

The regimental telephone was ringing when I raced back into
the barracks. "S-S-Sir," the operator stuttered, "there are bullets
coming through this building." Although he was very frightened
and confused, he stayed at his post. His action was one of many
examples of courage displayed by the fine young men serving our
country.

The destruction was devastating at Wheeler Field. When it

41

was obvious there was nothing left to destroy at the airfield, the enemy planes strafed the buildings at Schofield Barracks and dropped an occasional bomb on any likely looking target. This harassment continued for another two hours. We thought the Zeros would never go away. The concentration of fire, degree of destruction, and the number of casualties at Wheeler Field were second only to that inflicted on the Naval vessels at Pearl Harbor.

Most of the Army fighter planes were stationed at Wheeler Field, and the Japanese gave their destruction a high priority. However, two P-40 fighters, our newest, were parked on a small field located on the north shore of the island and thereby escaped the attack. They had been involved in target practice in the area and the pilots, Lieutenants Welch and Taylor to whom these two planes were assigned, had spent the night in Honolulu at a distance of about thirty miles from their planes. Nevertheless, during the attack these two young Lieutenants drove across the island to their planes and went aloft for combat. They were each credited with shooting down four Japanese planes.

Also spared in the attack were three P36 fighter planes located at Wheeler Field. They were parked some distance from the hangars and escaped detection by the Japanese pilots because of the dense smoke in that area. They were the only planes remaining that were operational. Our pilots managed to get aloft in these planes, and they shot down a few Japanese planes; however, one of the pilots was shot down and his body was never recovered from the water. In all, our pilots had ten confirmed Japanese plane kills and five other probable kills.

In spite of all the firing and billowing smoke from Pearl Harbor and Wheeler Field, which was clearly visible to us, it was difficult to believe that we were actually under hostile attack. In all of my military studies there had been nothing to tell me what to do in such a situation. Besides, we did not believe that such an attack by the Japanese was possible.

• The POA Defense •

Our alert status at this time had been concentrated against possible acts of sabotage. Our attempt to secure our facilities against sabotage was made difficult not only because it was not the policy of the high command to pass to subordinate units sensitive information, but also because the political situation was never discussed. As a result, our knowledge of security matters was limited to information provided by the news media. Consequently, I had read about the superior German Air Force but knew nothing concerning the threat of the Japanese to our safety other than possible sabotage.

What we actually did during this state of confusion and bewilderment was to go about our routine of issuing rifle ammunition and making preparations to move into our battle position, as though we were participating in a training exercise.

We experienced a considerable delay in executing orders for this move as our regimental commander, Colonel Adam Potts, lived off post. In the interim I ate breakfast and tried not to let the presence of an occasional bullet passing through the building disturb me. But the noise of a large plane approaching did prompt me to look out the window just in time to see a United States Army B-17 making a pass as if to land on the short parade ground alongside our dining room. This was one of the first of several B-17s arriving from the mainland of the United States. The condition of the airfield and the ongoing attack made their situation perilous, and each plane took individual action in an attempt to get on the ground. Many of them suffered various degrees of damage.

There had not been a concentrated attack against the buildings at Schofield barracks, and in spite of our vulnerability there and around the airfield, my unit suffered no casualties. One soldier raised up from his bed to see what was happening moments before a bullet went through his mattress another shot grazed the foot of a man nearby. After the virtual obliteration of Wheeler Field,

43

some planes still lingered behind the main attack force flying lazily over us in search of a likely target. On two occasions a bomb was dropped nearby but missed our personnel who were waiting in line to receive rifle ammunition. A continuous roar of rifle fire was directed at these planes, but they flew on without any apparent damage. Many of the planes flew so low we could clearly see the pilots, who appeared to be mocking us for our inability to stop them.

Even though we had no ammunition for our three-inch guns and our director (an antiquated machine which mechanically calculated firing data) was in the repair shop, we moved our unit into battle position near the end of one of the runways at Wheeler Field during the attack. In keeping with our conservative policies, ammunition for our big guns was kept in storage to preserve it from corrosion and deterioration. This central location was some distance away, resulting in a delay of several hours before we received ammunition.

Along the route to our battle position, we had a close-up view of the massive destruction at Wheeler Field. The bivouac where air personnel were housed was in shambles. If such a thing was possible, this destruction made us even more furious at the Japanese. Luckily there were very few men in the bivouac area at the time of the attack.

Our feelings were tempered somewhat by the local Japanese civilians who dropped to their knees and bowed to the ground as we passed them. The Japanese people, whether native, naturalized, or itinerant, loved Hawaii; however, they revered their roots and were saddened by the attack. Even so we were suspicious of any person of Japanese ancestry. Many of the local Japanese people had high-powered shortwave radios so they could receive programs from their homeland. These radios fed the rumors that the local Japanese were involved in sabotage and had assisted in the attack.

• The POA Defense •

Rifle ammunition had been issued to the troops, and our Communications Officer, Lieutenant Shaltsman, shot down one Japanese plane with his automatic rifle. The plane had just completed a strafing run across the airfield and was banking to make a turn when Saltsman's bullet hit the pilot in the head killing him instantly. The Zero hit the ground in a burst of flames at the edge of our position, and even though one airplane and one pilot wasn't much, it was at least something we could see. We felt a bit of satisfaction from his accomplishment, although, we were too busy organizing our position to give it the attention it deserved.

By the time the attack was over, we were in our assigned battle positions, and by noon we had ammunition for our three-inch guns. When we also received our mechanical firing data computer from the repair shop, we were finally ready to perform our primary mission of defense against enemy aircraft.

Included in our communications network was a line which continually sent information to us on the situation as it was collected and compiled from a central location. Hours after the Japanese planes had left we continued to receive such erroneous reports as "enemy planes approaching," "enemy paratroopers landing," and many other false reports. In fact, almost all of the reports we received were false. I began searching the sky like never before and spotted Venus near midday; until then I did not know that this was possible. As darkness approached, things became even more confused. Uncontrolled and almost uninterrupted gunfire from our own forces was coming from every direction.

At one point the message came through that my position was surrounded by enemy troops, and I had no reason to disbelieve the alert. As a result we were very tense and remained at our stations expecting to fire at any moment.

In the darkness we saw flashes of light at sea and shortly thereafter reports that our Naval Fleet was locked in battle with the Japanese began to come in. Days later I learned that this, too, was in error. We were told that the flashes of light we saw were lightning. Previously, I had been told that lightning never occurred in Hawaii, and I don't recall seeing any before or since this episode.

A token air and surface search was conducted by our Navy, but no visual contact of the attacking force was made. Even so, the fear that the Japanese would return stayed with us throughout the night. Sometime near midnight when planes from the aircraft carrier Enterprise came in to land, they were mistaken for the enemy. During this confusion, I received orders to place a barrage of antiaircraft fire into the air, and even though I knew there were no planes above my position, I was glad to receive the order. I felt that a few big booms from our guns would help relieve tension and would pose no danger to people in the area. Within minutes the report came over the wire that my position was being divebombed by the Japanese. This triggered a domino effect and almost immediately it seemed that all the other guns in the area began firing blindly in our direction. There were so many erroneous messages sent to us during the night that it appeared we were in a state of siege. At this point we had already endured some sixteen hours of terror so this incident did not seem too disturbing, and we took it in stride.

To be reduced from a state of peace and security to one of complete submission and mental defeat in such a short time was almost more than the mind could comprehend. Many personnel were not able to recover their stability and had to be returned to the States.

The shock seemed to be harder on the old line officers than on the younger ones. The older officers who had taught their art for so many years were not prepared for a type of warfare they knew nothing about. They could not fight the massive air strike. This left them not only stunned, but feeling like failures when they were unable to repel the attack. One of our Antiaircraft Battery Commanders became so confused he thought every plane he saw was Japanese. This happened in spite of the fact that airplane identification was emphasized in our training. He was relieved of his command as soon as his condition was recognized.

Throughout the night erroneous reports continued to come in, and the sporadic gunfire continued. I managed to nap a little until the early morning rain found its way into my folding cot, adding to my misery. As morning came the wild shooting stopped, but when darkness came again, so did the uncontrolled gunfire. This wild shooting was not deliberately aimed at anyone, and no casualties were reported because of it; however, it was disconcerting as well as frightening to say the least. Order was restored slowly, so that we gained enough confidence in our local security to sleep without a gun in our hands after a while.

Two days after the attack, I received orders to move my unit to a position on Pearl Peninsula. At this location, we were able to improve our comfort, but on more than one occasion, we drew machinegun fire from our own destroyers anchored in the harbor near us. Night after night we were alerted by numerous reports of unidentified planes approaching the area. We manned our guns in preparation to fire at any potential target but the aircraft always proved to be our own. In fact, the only enemy plane to fly over Hawaii after December 7 was a small Japanese pontoon plane which was launched from a submarine some distance off shore. The bomb it dropped in a wooded area near Honolulu did not inflict any significant damage.

Pearl Peninsula which juts into Pearl Harbor was inhabited by civilians, adding to the problem of local security. Maintaining an adequate perimeter defense required the use of many soldiers. We had to use a lot of troops having no previous experience and little or no knowledge of the automatic weapons assigned to them. As a result, we had to indulge in some fast on-the-job training.

• An Eyewitness Account •

Pulling together in this manner helped to restore some of the confidence that earlier seemed to have been mortally wounded by the Japanese attack. It seemed we had too little time in a day to accomplish the necessary things, to achieve excellence in our ability to perform. Nevertheless a sense of urgency motivated us to push ahead.

4

ADJUSTING TO THE WAYS AND MEANS OF WAR

Slowly we adjusted to our new way of living and even regained some of our previous comforts. We installed a shower head in a former pig feed lot near our improvised temporary shelters. As time passed, I was amazed at how fast the men were able to adjust to new environments.

Memories of home were sparked by the *Panama Clipper,* a large flying boat, which used the waters between our position and Ford Island to take off and land in its scheduled flights to and from the States. This event became the highlight of my day as it was a comfort to look at the plane and to think that in a few short hours it would be in the U.S.A. I did not allow myself to think that I might never return to the States, even though I feared I might not.

Meanwhile our Navy made great strides in rebuilding the naval armada. Soon, limited combat was undertaken in the Central Pacific areas. Dry dock for ship repairs was a short distance across a span of water from my battery, and after each naval battle the crippled ships would hobble in for repairs. I knew many of the pilots who were stationed aboard the carriers through social contacts at the Officers Clubs prior to the Japanese attack. They were the older, more seasoned officers, and it was alarming to discover how many of them did not return to port with the carriers they had sailed out on.

It was at this point, when our naval strength was so terribly-weakened, that our top commanders learned of the attack the Japanese planned to launch on Midway Island. The early success of the Japanese forces induced them to go for a bold stroke they hoped would eventually include their occupation of the Hawaiian Islands. The big island of Hawaii was their first objective.

The attack on Pearl Harbor caused a reorganization of Antiaircraft Artillery command structure. The old Regimental-Battalion-Battery organization was dropped and replaced with the group battery type unit. The group headquarters was more versatile in that as few or as many Batteries needed for any mission could be attached to it. It adapted to wartime needs well and was designed for such purposes. The group headquarters plan also cut down on the number of officers and enlisted men needed for administrative duties. Such was the case for most combat units. Along with this restructure of organization, many of the career senior officers were moved to locations where their services were most needed. Some went to the European theater of the war, and reserve officers were moved up to replace them. I was complimented to be the first officer in my category to be moved.

In April 1942, I was transferred to the Antiaircraft group headquarters for the Pearl Harbor area. My assignment was Executive Officer with the rank of captain. Shortly thereafter I was moved to Kaneoha Bay AAA group headquarters, because of a special need there. As it happened, one of the AAA units had fired into a residential area during a practice firing. Although no casualties resulted, this error was embarrassing to the AAA commander. Because of the reputation I had gained as an excellent gunnery officer and budding entrepreneur, I was selected for the trouble-shooting assignment of mending fences between the military and civilian population.

In May 1942, there was an air of urgency in the Hawaiian Islands, and although only a few people knew the real cause, we were well aware of the Japanese threat. Units were brought up to full strength with new men, most of whom had only basic training and no knowledge of the weapons to which they were assigned.

• The POA Defense •

We noted that many Army landbased bombers as well as many Navy bombers were being moved in. The place was a beehive of activity. It wasn't long before we learned the reason—the impending battle of Midway.

Some of the landbased bombers had been sent on to Midway where they were parked and camouflaged while others were stationed at strategic advance locations. These bombers were to employ the new skip bombing technique which required a low level dropping of bombs to the water in such a way so that they would skip along to their targets like a thrown rock. This new strategy played a big part in turning the tide against the Japanese Navy.

Our victory at the battle of Midway was so unexpected and so complete that the Japanese changed many of their war plans, including their plan to take the Aleutian Islands and Hawaii. Their landing forces withdrew without any attempt to land on Midway.

It was about this time that I received my first opportunity to return to the States. New Army Antiaircraft Artillery regiments were being formed for deployment in the European theater and I was invited by one of the new regimental commanders, Colonel John Mitchell, to join him as part of his staff. This appealed to me greatly but I realized that the stay in the States would be brief so I turned down the invitation. Also, I was beginning to feel that good things were ahead for me where I was.

My duties in Kaneoha Bay were not strenuous, and for the first time since the attack on Pearl Harbor there was time for sports and relaxation. I lived in the Naval Bachelor Officers Quarters where I had most of the comforts of home, as well as good food in the cafeteria. Somehow the Navy seemed to have better rations than the Army and I enjoyed them. The Officers Club was across the street, and occasionally on weekends we had time to attend parties with the nurses from a nearby hospital.

Our command post was in an underground concrete storage

51

building near my quarters. It was necessary to have at least one officer on duty twentyfour hours a day, but usually the entire staff was there in the evenings, including the duty officer. Not only was it a good place for us to relax and have fellowship, but it was also easier to observe the blackouts in this pleasant surrounding.

Our group doctor had at one time played with a nationally famous band, and under his guidance we formed a small combo. With a great deal of patience he taught each of us to play an instrument. All instruments were of the stringed variety, and I played a four-stringed tenor guitar. The quality of our music may have left much to be desired, but this did not detract from our fun. On one occasion we even played for a local wedding. The duration of this combo was short because of the transfers which regularly took our members away to other locations, and it saddened all of us when we lost a player.

The music helped our snug command post develop into a popular place where many VIPs came in the evenings. Some of the best hours were spent there with the author Edgar Rice Burroughs, who was a civilian assigned to Special Services. He captivated us all with his easy, warm manner as he sat and chatted with us throughout many evenings. Although he loved to sip his Scotch whiskey, he never drank enough to affect his stability. His Tarzan stories had always been a favorite of mine, so I was surprised to learn that Mr. Burroughs had never seen a jungle.

At the end of these sessions, when the visitors departed, the duty officer was left alone with the mice for the rest of the night. In time the mice became so tame they would eat out of our hand and so helped us to pass the lonely nights.

Kaneoha Bay was the base for PBY flying boats, and these planes were used for reconnaissance flights far out from the islands. The PBY pilots lived in the same Bachelor Officers Quarters where I lived, so naturally I got to know these men fairly well. When a plane did not return from its mission, I always felt a keen sense of loss.

• The POA Defense •

Pilots were a special breed and there was always a shortage of them. Consequently, training was cut short, and new pilots were frequently sent into combat with fewer than forty hours flight training. I recall one occasion when a large group of new Navy pilots arrived en route for service aboard an aircraft carrier. Many of these men had never seen an aircraft carrier, and they were on their way to make their first carrier landing. After a brief stopover at the base, they bravely flew off to their assigned carrier, which was already at sea, and I never saw any of them again. I often wondered how many of them made that first landing and how many went into the sea.

The Kaneoha Bay airfield was used extensively by carrier based Navy planes for practice landings and as an operational base for practice divebombing. Once, my desire to experience the sensation of divebombing led me to fly a mission with one of these pilots. We took off with two other planes and climbed to ten thousand feet, while a short distance offshore a target was being towed for their use. We arrived over the target and headed almost straight down in our dive at full throttle. My heart was in my throat when it looked like we were going to slam into the target, but at the last moment the pilot leveled off to drop his practice missiles. He repeated this routine several times, and even though I gained a new respect for these dare devils of the sky, I was glad when it was over. The rapid change in altitude felt like two sharp sticks were being pushed through my head from either side. The pain was almost unbearable. The results were one bleeding ear and a rather messy case of airsickness. "Never again," I asserted.

The pilot told me that as a result of the practice nature fortified them for rapid change in air pressure by causing their ear drums to increase in thickness. It didn't seem to work for me.

I gained even more respect for pilots when I had an opportunity to go aboard the aircraft carrier *Enterprise* during a training mission at sea. The pilots were doing practice landings, and I was amazed at how rough the landings were. The impact of the airplanes on the deck was so severe I was surprised that the planes did not fall apart. Although, to tell the truth, many of them did sustain some damage. Even the most experienced pilot admitted that landings were hazardous, and they were apprehensive about making them. I didn't have an opportunity to make one of these landings, but it was just as well since merely watching them made my teeth hurt.

I do recall a flight aboard a B-17 bomber which occured somewhat after this test and caused quite a stir, however. We had gone far out to sea to test the detection efficiency of the radar network on Oahu. The pilot brought us back at an altitude of twenty thousand feet with our friendly aircraft signal turned off. Our plane was picked up by shore based radar and was immediately given unidentified status. I was overwhelmed with the fear every crew member of a bomber or fighter plane must face at the prospect of being shot down. I had gained a new respect for God by the time our pilot established our true identity, and we were safely on the ground.

Our radar system had many flaws and often gave false alarms as with the case of the "Ghost of Kaneoha." Almost nightly our AAA radar would detect what appeared to be a surface vessel moving aimlessly a short distance off shore. After a time, it would disappear from the radar screen like an enemy submarine. With no positive evidence that anything was actually out there the naval commander of the base felt we should try to sight the mysterious craft. The commander and I decided that we would go out to the area in late evening in a small boat and drift in silence to wait for the imaginary submarine to surface. We were to maintain radio silence but would keep our receiving sets on for information from shore. As the last glimmer of light faded, we began scanning the surface with our binoculars. Hours passed with no evidence of any object other than our own craft in the area. So far all we had gotten for our efforts was a severe case of seasickness. After a while, we found ourselves slowly drifting on a collision course with a high rock formation near the entrance to the channel and were forced to abandon our mission and head for shore. On our way back, we heard over the radio that the radar had picked up an unidentified surface vessel entering the harbor channel and realized it was us. When we continued to receive the same information over and over, we realized our sending set was not getting through. I decided we were between one of those proverbial rocks and a hard place. On the one hand, we stood the danger of being mistaken for an enemy ship, and on the other hand, the enemy could be in the area. The chance that we could be caught between friendly and unfriendly fire did not do much to soothe my nerves. Just when I was beginning to think I would never make it to actual combat, we finally were able to identify ourselves by blinking a light: the sense of relief which came over me was so potent that it left me weak. Even though we failed to spot the ghost ship, I was very grateful to get back to shore. We decided to use other methods to detect the ghost. In this effort I was not trying to be heroic, I was simply attempting to solve a mystery.

The Kaneoha Bay area was defended by large mobile seacoast guns, heavy field artillery, and antiaircraft weapons. Certainly there was enough firepower to protect us against any invading vessel real or imagined. Our next move was to construct a fire control board that would enable us to fire all of these weapons from several units at once towards a point where we had determined the "ghost" to be located. On the night we scheduled for this blowout, the Commanders of the heavy artillery units came to our Command Post and each Commander established telephone communications with his respective fire unit. When our ghost appeared on the radar screens we started our tracking operation. Excitement grew as each Commander began feeding location data to his respective unit. Finally, we were going to put all of our training to use. In moments we would all be firing our weapons at an enemy target for the first time. Once a pattern of movement had been established by the ghost, we selected a point ahead as our target and calculated the precise moment when the ghost would arrive at that point. All clocks were synchronized to facilitate firing all weapons at the proper time for the projectiles to arrive on target at precisely the same moment. Months and years had been spent in training for such a moment, and our operations room was alive with excitement as the Commanders hurriedly transmitted data to their units. Almost like an Olympian who after years of strenuous training is about to perform for the first time in competition for a gold medal, these officers had arrived at an exciting and crucial moment in their careers.

When the smoke had cleared and the noise had faded nothing was on the radar screen and the ocean was as peaceful as ever. In due time our ghost was determined to be a reflection from the mountains located to the rear of our radar set. This radar was similar to the ones that had been used at the time of the attack on Pearl Harbor and were not very accurate. It was understandable why the operators had no firm conclusions about what they were observing on their screens. The imperfect machines hollered wolf so often that on that occasion of December 7, 1941, the unsuspecting operators did not realize that the Japanese attack was for real.

5

HEADQUARTERS UNITED STATES ARMY FORCES PACIFIC OCEAN AREA

One of the first things I did after my move to the Kaneoha group headquarters in April of 1942 was to make an appraisal of the antiaircraft artillery batteries to determine their needs for better performance. I found the units needed more training. In addition to the type of training normally introduced, to increase proficiency I taught the batteries to fire on unseen surface targets. When Major General Henry T. Burgin, commanding general of the artillery command, learned about this, he came over to view a demonstration.

We climbed atop an observation tower for a good view of the water area where the Navy was pulling a target for us. But when I saw the target, I was shocked to see that the short tow line gave us very little room for error. My order for the units to commence tracking and fire when ready was given reluctantly and with crossed fingers. It was soon very obvious that the many hours of training paid off. I felt my chest swell with pride as each man did his job smoothly, and the target was hit. The real reward came when General Burgin turned to me with his penetrating eyes and asked; "Well, Smith, how do you feel about their demonstration?"

I replied, "Just shows what good training can do." He quickly turned to leave and said in passing, "That's what I think, too."

This was in late November of 1942, and orders were issued immediately for my transfer to Major General Burgin's staff. This move was a part of a continuing plan to replace many of the professional career officers for duties in higher command positions elsewhere. Many of these officers were sent to the European theatre of operations.

My duties included the responsibility to advise and consult with, the commanding general on all matters concerning the AAA. In this position it was essential to be knowledgeable in every facet of the use of antiaircraft artillery weapons.

Our combined headquarters staff compiled complete plans for all assault operations and maintained plans for probable action far in advance of the actual assaults. In many respects these young officers (mostly majors and colonels) directed the war. The responsibilities were great, and a mistake in judgement meant an immediate transfer.

The first real important assignment I had was to make a study on the advisability of keeping the barrage balloon unit as a part of the air defense of Pearl Harbor. My studies in military science taught me how to present such a study—the pros and cons are impartially presented, followed by analysis and conclusion. Most of my reference material was written by the British and taken from reports they made during the defense of London early in World War II. These reports indicated that the deterrent factor of the balloons was more mental than actual. Then, too, it restricted our own planes from the use of the area. My recommendation was to discontinue their use. Within a few days they were permanently removed. This success was a new experience for me, and perhaps made me a little heady at the realization of the power my decisions had.

I could hardly believe the attention I began to receive from brigadier generals of subordinate commands. It was "Hello Bill" from generals who had never before known me. Of course, I knew it wasn't me they were catering to, but rather they were acknowledging the power of Major General Burgin behind me. Even so, I couldn't help feeling important.

Each staff member had to take his turn as night duty officer for the area command headquarters. As duty officer we were immediately informed of unusual activity in the area, and, if need be, we were expected to make decisions for the commanding general. My first thoughts were "How can they place such important decisions on the shoulders of a little man from Owl Creek?" My ego was fed even more when, on rare occasions, I stood in at official functions for General Burgin, the Military Governor.

It was 1942, and our headquarters was located deep underground near Fort Shafter at the Army-Air Force control center. The duty there was pretty comfortable and during my turn as officer-of-the-day there was always a cot neatly prepared with fresh white linen. I went to bed at a normal hour and was only disturbed when a real need existed.

Though we did have comforts there were also drawbacks from being in these underground positions. One was an unusual odor of wet lime which clung to everything, and because of the lack of sunlight we had to be supplied with Vitamin D pills. Inasmuch as about half of my time was spent away from the underground office, I did not feel a real need for the pills but took them anyway.

We played softball to counteract the lack of sunlight and exercise. General Clark Ruffner, who became the commanding general of the United States forces in South Korea, was the pitcher in many of these games and I was the catcher. We also played tennis on a court belonging to our neighbors, the Dillinghams.

By 1943 the allied forces were still on the defensive and most of my time was consumed with inspections of artillery units to determine if they were capable of performing their mission in defense against enemy aircraft. My job was to arrive at an antiaircraft artillery unit unannounced and alert them to prepare for action against a simulated target. The test was not extensive, but it was always effective and conclusive.

• An Eyewitness Account •

My first inspection was of search light units and I found them in such a bad state of readiness that it was doubtful they could perform as expected. My report was sent by endorsement of the artillery commanding general to the commanding general, headquarters of AAA for correction and report. When the report was returned to our headquarters with the notation that deficiencies had been corrected, General Burgin said, "Smith, let's go take a look to verify the condition."

When we arrived at the same unit and found that the deficiencies had not been corrected, the General's action was swift. He wrote a smoking letter to General Perkins, the commanding general of headquarters Antiaircraft Artillery Command. He also instructed me to "hit" every searchlight unit in the command.

I found they were all equally bad except the last unit. I knew this battery commander and was aware of his outstanding record so it was no surprise that this particular unit was in excellent condition. In my report I detailed the superior condition of the unit and commended its commanding officer, Captain John Preston Pittman. Because of this report Captain Pittman was transferred into the AAA headquarters command post and promoted to Major.

Captain Pittman had been my roommate in college, and even though we both had a good laugh about this incident, we dared not reveal our friendship. This might have been classed as a conflict of interest. All the same Captain Pittman was an excellent officer and deserved recognition for what I had accurately reported. It also gave me a chance to repay him for the many times in college when I was short of money that he brought me food from the dormitory cafeteria where he worked.

A real plum in my assignment was when Major General Henry T. Burgin, my immediate boss, invited me to move into the so-called "Burgin Manor" with him and his other staff members. The Burgin Manor was, a multi-million dollar estate located on

• The POA Defense •

Waikiki Beach at the point of Diamond Head. It was owned by Mr. Henry T. Fagin, who owned sugar cane operations on the Hawaiian island of Molokai and in California.

The Fagin estate came equipped with servants, grounds keepers and a superb wine cellar. The cellar was off limits to us, but on special occasions Mr. Fagin would instruct General Burgin to draw from its stock of fine champagne.

All the servants were of Japanese extraction, but there was no doubt about their loyalty. Shizu, the Japanese lady in charge, had no children and became very attached to us. She instinctively knew when we were on a combat mission and worried about us until we returned. Saverino, our Filipino cook, was General Burgin's personal cook whom he had picked up in the Philippines when he served as Commander of the Philippine forces. Saverino's culinary art was incomparable. No one else, including Admiral Chester W. Nimitz, enjoyed such luxury.

Frequently General Burgin would invite high officers of the Command to dine with us, and it soon became a status symbol to receive such an invitation to the Manor. We felt honored on the occasions that Admiral Nimitz dined with us. These parties did not occur very often, but, during my thirty month stay, they added up to several memorable occasions. We could relax and let our hair down a bit but were still reminded of our staff positions and maintained a certain amount of control. We knew that to violate our code of conduct meant an early transfer. In fact, I remember only one episode that came close to a breach in discipline.

It had been a normal evening even though we all had lady guests which meant the Manor was filled with laughter and gaiety. After dinner we had gathered at the piano to reminisce and sing songs popular at the time. Later in the evening the General and his guest, an Army nurse, wandered outside to the pool where the nurse, much to the General's delight, proceeded to jump in. This impulsive action lit the fuse, and in no time we were all in the pool.

• An Eyewitness Account •

The men had their swim suits but the women had to improvise with towels or whatever was at hand. As some of their makeshift suits were very imaginative and provocative, it turned into a very memorable evening.

Life at the Burgin Manor was not all fun and games. In some respects we felt like we were always living at attention with no real time to relax. The best break in our routine was an inspection tour of the other islands.

One such inspection tour in April 1943 took Lieutenant Colonel Nick Carter and me to Midway Island. Marine and Naval units were responsible for the defense of this island, which meant that our staff had no direct responsibility there. However, Admiral "Beauty" Martin, the Island Commander, asked that we make a courtesy evaluation of his defenses.

Midway lies about eleven hundred miles west of Oahu, Hawaii. Because it is an atoll, Midway is one of my favorite Pacific islands: that it is purported to have the most comfortable climate in the Pacific helps, of course. The width of the island generally is only about one thousand feet while its length is about five miles. Although it has no well-defined lagoon, the center section of the island is submerged in such a way that it forms what might be called two islands.

I learned a great deal about the island during this trip. Midway Island was used before World War II as a Service Center for the Transoceanic Cable. When the war started operation of the cable system was discontinued and all civilian maintenance personnel were evacuated allowing the Navy to occupy the vacated buildings.

Admiral Martin lived there in a very attractive house and invited Nick and me to his house for dinner. We were served a marvelous five-course dinner by his Philippine cook in an uptown style.

Later that afternoon we were out for a walk and had a chance to observe one of the dress codes practiced by the men on the island. Our attention was called to this when we had to step aside to allow an open-bodied truck loaded with Marines to pass. The truck stopped close to the beach, and I had to blink my eyes when the tailgate fell down, and about two dozen Marines tumbled out each as naked as the day he was born. This totally relaxed dress code was allowed only because there were no women on the island. To say the least, it gave the men a chance to get an all around tan.

My knowledge of the island would not have been complete without learning something about the wildlife it supported. Because of the dense groves of tall eucalyptus trees and lush tropical plants, Midway is host to many exotic birds. In particular, I remember one beautiful white bird with pink eyes because it seemed to be very curious about us. It would hover about three to four feet over our heads and look us over. The unique thing about this bird was that it seemed to have no feet. When on the ground it would pull itself along with its bill and for sanctuary at night it would crawl into a hole in the ground. Although, I had neither seen nor heard of this bird before going to Midway, I had heard of the native albatross or gooney bird. The adult female of this species hollows out a place in the sand near trees and hatches two young birds. The chicks are covered with white down and grow to be so fat they are as large as a goose. Finally the mother leaves them to fend for themselves and migrates to the Alaskan Aleutian Islands for the summer. The abandoned chicks, with no one to feed them, trim down to about the size of a small duck and are then able to head for the beach to forage for food. They remain grounded until they gain strength in their long wings and can take to the air. It was a delight to watch as they accidentally became airborne in play, and when they realized what had happened, they seemed to panic and fold their wings to come tumbling to the ground. They did this many times before finally learning to fly. These birds must take off into the wind much like an airplane. On many occasions we were able to catch these beautiful creatures but we always released them unharmed.

I was reminded of the terrible reality of war by the incredible battle scars left on this peaceful landscape by the battle fought over it. I noticed its facade of beauty and peace was further marred when I visited our most forward naval submarine base and talked to some of the sailors. They enthusiastically related stories of their patrols. One of their greatest enjoyments had been sinking fishing boats and then conducting target practice against the survivors. I remember feeling my stomach churn as I wondered how young men could have become so cruel and callous in such a short time.

6

A VISIT HOME

In October 1943, General Burgin announced that our staff would take turns returning to the mainland to inspect new armament and take a six-week refresher course in our particular branch of service. Most of us had been in the Pacific area for two or more years without a break, and this news was viewed as a much needed vacation. The length of time seemed much longer when one considers the fact that our position was so demanding that we hardly knew when Christmas or any other normal holiday passed. Duty seemed more like a never-ending day and as most of us had forgotten what a normal life was like we eagerly awaited our turn to go home.

Sometimes I would stop by the Moana Hotel to hear the program "Hawaii Calls," which was being beamed to the United States, and the mere thought that some of my family were possibly listening to the same music somehow seemed to put me in touch with them. Loneliness was a constant companion, and anything could spark it. At times even a glance at the moon would fill me with longing when I would think someone from home might be looking at the same moon. Then finally the day arrived when we took Nick to Hickam Field for his flight to California where his wife and family would be waiting for him. We were excited almost to the point of foolishness when we saw him off.

This excitement continued during the trip back to the manor, and as I ran from the Jeep to the back entrance, I fell and sprained my ankle. The pop was so loud that everyone heard it, including General Burgin, who was waiting just inside the house. I hobbled inside and sat down where the General was waiting. He helped me to a chair, then removed my shoes, and rubbed my ankle. I was touched by his compassion, and the thought crossed my mind that here was the most feared Army general in the Pacific on his knees in front of a junior officer. This was a side of him I had never seen, and it only strengthened my respect for him. He saw that I got to the hospital where my injury was diagnosed as a severe sprain and after an overnight stay I returned to duty.

Following Colonel Carter's departure, it was my turn for a vacation. In November of 1943, I flew to San Francisco where I boarded a train for Camp Davis, North Carolina, interrupted by a much needed stopover at home in Memphis, Tennessee. Contrary to what I had thought, the never-to-be trip home was actually happening. From St. Louis, Missouri, I telephoned my home to let my family know that I would arrive in Memphis in the early hours of the morning. By the treatment I received on my trip across country I learned that any Pearl Harbor survivor was considered a VIP. One porter even asked if he could touch me and refused a tip.

Several members of my family were at the station to meet me, and when I saw them from the window my eyes started burning with tears. I was in such a state of excitement when I got off the train that sometime later I realized that in my heightened joy I could not recall who met me.

All too soon it was January 1944, and I was back in San Francisco ready to set sail for Hawaii. My visit home was more gratifying than I could have imagined. For that short time, the war was far away, and I was able to relax. After leaving my family and friends again, I discovered I was even more committed to my assignment, and there was new vigor in my purpose.

7

UNITED STATES FORCES MAKE THEIR MOVE

In preparation for our offensive moves against the Japanese in what we called "island hopping," there was a reorganization of command structure. Headquarters Pacific Ocean Areas was formed and to accommodate our planned push to the home islands of Japan I was moved on up to the Army forces portion of this Headquarters. General Burgin was moved up to Commanding General, Central Pacific Area, and even though I was no longer on General Burgin's staff I continued to live at the Burgin Manor.

My main duty as a member of the joint Army-Navy Board for Air Defense was to assist in writing and maintaining a standing operating procedure for air defense during the assault and occupation of an island. Other duties shifted from inspections of units to planning for future operations. It was my staff responsibility to design the preliminary plan for antiaircraft defense on all islands, designated or planned for occupation including Japan and China. Also, I maintained a list of Antiaircraft Artillery units to be used in these defenses. In anticipation of the end of hostilities in Europe, many of these units would have to be moved in from another theater for the final phases.

The final planning for an operation would start with an announcement from the War Department Joint Chiefs of Staff in Washington that we would conduct an assault on Island X, date Y, and that the Navy would provide for Z tons of shipping. Immediately all staff members involved would be called together and instructed to compile a list of the number and type of units needed in their category and the total tonnage of shipping required. This was made easier by one practice of having contingency plans ready far in advance.

• An Eyewitness Account •

As expected, the total tonnage of shipping needed was sometimes as much as double the space available and created the
problem of having to strip down. There were two ways to do this:
cut down on the number of units and/or reduce the size of the
units. We usually did both. In a latter phase of movement, units
would be brought back to normal strength. With a trial and error
approach, we arrived at the number and types of units to be used.
We were then ready to issue the necessary instructions to the
designated units. For security reasons, only key men were told
where and when the assault would be.

It was an unwritten rule in our artillery staff that one member
would accompany the assault troops on each operation as an
observer and write an operational report of the action. The elected
man would move in with a unit of the assault force a few days
before embarkation. The first operation was the island of Tarawa
in June of 1944, and the job of observer fell to me. However,
Baker Island was scheduled to be occupied a few days prior to
Tarawa in order to provide for a close land support base, and I
accompanied the task force as an observer.

Baker, an island one mile in diameter, lies three miles above
the equator and southeast of Tarawa, Gilbert Islands. It had no
lagoon, and a flat skyline which was broken by the one tree on the
island. Baker was a nesting island for the sea birds which were so
numerous they hardly had standing room and posed a threat to
aircraft taking off and landing.

The number one mission of the task force was to construct a
landing strip, using a product called the "Marston Mat." The
actual construction was simple. Bulldozers leveled the sand and
engineers laid down the honeycombed metal plates of the "Martson
Mat" which would turn the better part of the small island into an
airfield.

There were no Japanese troops on Baker Island, and our only
contact with them was through their reconnaissance planes. On

the first day in the area, our carrier-based planes surprised and shot down a Japanese reconnaissance plane. The following day another enemy plane was detected, and this plane was also shot down. However, as three passes were required to finish the job, we felt that its radio operator had sufficient time to report the encounter. Three days later, two enemy planes were spotted, and again our carrier planes went after them. One plane was shot down and the second plane was damaged but managed to escape. We were now reasonably sure the Japanese knew about our presence and so we increased our lookout. We felt pressured to get the landing field finished so we could give the neighboring islands the protection of fighter planes and a land base for our navy bombers to use in the assault on Tarawa.

As soon as the Japanese learned of our presence on Baker Island, they discontinued their reconnaissance flights and never challenged us in any way. Furthermore, due to the overwhelming defeat at Midway, the Japanese navy did not again oppose us in force until we reached the Mariana Islands.

Most of the garrison personnel were transported to Baker Island on the *USS President Tyler*. On this trip in June, 1944 I was fortunate to meet, and get to know, Commander Black. He and I shared a stateroom aboard the *USS President Tyler* then shared a tent after we went ashore. Commander Black had been a member of Admiral Richard E. Byrd's party in the South Pole expedition in 1929. Interestingly, he had been in charge of the group that established a runway on Howland Island for Amelia Earhart's flight around the world, an island located only about 35 miles northwest of Baker.

Commander Black's assignment was to go to Howland Island by small surface craft and see what the situation was there. As we talked about Earhart's fate, he told me that on July 2, 1937 he attempted to steer Mrs. Earhart in for a landing on that fateful day, but she was hopelessly lost. He talked to her on the radio throughout the ordeal and her last words were, "We are out of gas and are going down." It was encounters such as this one with Commander Black which reaffirm the historic character of the men and women who fought in the Pacific.

Canton Island is located about three hundred miles southeast of Baker Island, and our forces there were under the command of Colonel Kenneth Barrager, a close personal friend and former Commanding Officer of my antiaircraft artillery group at Kaneoha Naval Base. Consequently, I found it convenient while in the area to go by and make an inspection of his defenses. He put on a demonstration of his capabilities, and my formal report was highly complimentary. His outstanding accomplishments there were so impressive, he was eventually brought back to Hawaii and given the assignment of commander antiaircraft artillery landing and garrison forces for Saipan.

After two days at Canton Island, I flew back to Hawaii via Christmas and Palmyra Islands. Palmyra is a beautiful atoll with many coconut palms which lies about 800 miles south of Hawaii. On this trip aboard a Navy flying boat, we landed on Palmyra to refuel. Shortly after takeoff, we encountered a squall so severe the pilot lowered his plane to only a few feet above the water. I remembered that this was where Captain Eddie Rickenbacker had gone down just a short time earlier. The Pacific is known for these sudden violent storms, and I felt certain that I was about to be lost at sea. With the blessings of luck and a skilled pilot, we made it through the storm suffering neither damage to the aircraft or ourselves. These little breaks from the planning board and inspections tours were always welcome and never failed to "stir my juices," as the pilots used to say.

Sometime prior to our assault on Tarawa the Navy made a pass through the area and bombarded several of the islands with battleships and carrier-based planes. They came back very exuberant and said we should have had our troops along because, they could have walked ashore with ease. From aloft, or at a distance, the effects of such a concentrated attack looked devastating and those participating often had an exaggerated opinion of how damaging their fire really was. For instance, when the landing of Tarawa was scheduled, these same forces bombarded Tarawa for several days, yet we lost one thousand men in the assault. The Japanese were dug in so well that ground troops were the only way to get to them. Bombing would certainly shake them up, but it could not destroy the caves and bunkers the Japanese had so painstakingly constructed.

When the Japanese fortified these islands, they did so with no intention of ever surrendering. Colonel Ernest V. Holmes, Operations Officer U. S. Army Forces Pacific Ocean Areas related an amusing but meaningful incident after his return from Kwajalein Island of the Marshall Islands Operation, February 1944. The siege was virtually over when down on the tip of the island where a handful of Japanese remained, one called out, "You Yankees give up, we be good to you." This was an example of the unique philosophy of the Japanese soldier. The word "surrender" does not exist in their own discipline.

8

FRANKLIN D. ROOSEVELT
VISITS HAWAII

In the midst of campaigning for his fourth term, President Roosevelt came to Hawaii. A special war room was set up for this occasion with maps and all the visual aids necessary to present to the President both our military situation and the projection of our planned push to Japan. Things were happening fast in the combat area, and it was a busy time for commanders and their staffs. The deadline was approaching for a leap forward in General Douglas A. MacArthur's South Pacific Area, as well as in our own Pacific Ocean Area. Prior to this meeting, the decision had been made to consign General MacArthur the Philippine Islands from our Pacific Ocean Areas command. This was also rehearsed for President Roosevelt.

General MacArthur was summoned to Hawaii for this occasion. Because he was a former West Point classmate and longtime friend of General Burgin, General Burgin had met him at the plane. Afterwards, he told us that he had never seen General MacArthur so mad and that MacArthur felt he had been forced to leave his command post at a critical time for no purpose other than politics.

His displeasure was apparent during the presentation in the war room and came to a head after one of President Roosevelt's interruptions to make a comment of his own. General MacArthur's patience was finally exhausted, and he turned to the President and remarked in his well-known manner, "Sometimes I wondah where you get all of your misinformation."

After a cursory presentation of the war situation the meeting

73

was adjourned, and President Roosevelt was escorted on a tour of Oahu with Colonel Holmes of our staff leading the way.

I discovered after this incident that General Burgin, one of the most intelligent men I have ever known, had very few good things to say about the President. However, after Mrs. Eleanor Roosevelt followed the President with a visit, General Burgin classified her among the most intelligent women he had known. Personal opinions were not normally aired by those attending high level conferences, but General Burgin privately kept us posted on most matters of mutual interest in such meetings.

9

JAPANESE BOMB OUR WEST COAST AREAS

From the Fall of 1944 to the Spring of 1945, the Japanese launched an estimated fifteen thousand paper balloons into the jet stream destined for the West Coast of the United States. Each balloon was armed with explosive and incendiary bombs. The balloons were thirty-two feet in diameter and contained controls which kept them at altitudes of thirty thousand to thirty-five thousand feet, where favorable winds up to two hundred miles an hour were likely to take them to our West Coast areas. Upon their arrival, a timer was scheduled to open a valve allowing the hydrogen to escape permitting the balloons to fall. Many of these balloons reached their target area causing minor damage and a few casualties. Because the news of their success was a well-kept secret from the enemy, the Japanese concluded that the bombs were not reaching their target and discontinued the operation. Occasionally, the jet stream would swing south far enough to bring the balloons into radar range of Hawaii where they were intercepted by our Air Corps and shot out of the sky. Our leaders classified the balloons as only a minor harassment and did nothing other than this to neutralize them.

10

THE MARIANA ISLANDS

In rapid succession, our forces captured strategic islands of the Gilbert, Caroline, Marshall, and Mariana chains. Saipan, populated mainly by civilians, and the native Chamorro who were the minority inhabitants, was the first of these islands to fall. The plan was to launch an assault on Guam, also in the Marianas, as soon as it could be determined that the required forces would not be needed at Saipan. Following the seizure of Guam and Saipan, the other Mariana Islands, Rota and Tinian, were to be taken. My assignment was to accompany the assault forces on the Saipan operation.

The assault force for Saipan consisted of three Marine divisions and one Army division. Marine General, Holland M. (Howling Mad) Smith was the assault force Commander. For staging, I was attached to a Marine Artillery Battalion located on the island of Maui, Hawaii. Shortly after my arrival in the staging area, we boarded a transport that was anchored offshore. From there we conducted a practice landing on the nearby beaches before moving to Honolulu Harbor to become part of a task force consisting of approximately 500 Naval ships. Escort vessels, including destroyers and small aircraft carriers, were a part of the convoy, and as we moved deeper into enemy waters the numbers and types of escort vessels were increased. A mock-up of the island of Saipan was constructed on the deck for war games simulations. During the day I spent a great deal of time observing these training sessions. As an observer my only assignment was to monitor the action and write a report; so this left me with a lot of idle time, and I had to look for activities to ward off boredom.

• An Eyewitness Account •

During the daylight hours, I discovered planes from the aircraft carriers maintained a continuous surveillance of our convoy and the surrounding area. Watching the varied activities required to maintain these flights kept me entertained for awhile. Even this routine was interrupted for about four days by incessant rains when we were between the northern and southern trade winds. We were in this area when we received news of the allied landing at Normandy Beach in France. This news held our interest through the confinement of the rainy spell.

During this time I discovered I was a pretty fair poker player and made a friend of an artillery battery commander who really loved his cards. He was always ready for a game and looked at life in the same manner as he played cards. He felt he could manage anything the cards turned up and was so positive and sure about what life would deal him. He was convinced that he had control of all the cards and nothing would happen to him. His attitude was so strong that I was also convinced he was indestructible. When I got the news that he lost his life early in the landing operation, I felt an emptiness that stayed with me for a long time. I was so sure that he would make it back home that I had to face the possibility that maybe I would not make it either.

The entire convoy pulled into the lagoon at Eniwetok Island in the Marshall chain. At this point, I transferred to the command ship. I thought Eniwetok was one of the most interesting of the atoll islands. The lagoon has a diameter of about twenty miles and the coral reef submerges in many places to form several small islets that vary in width from a few feet to about five hundred. The most interesting attraction was at the island Base Exchange where the only woman on the island was employed. She was attractive, personable and naturally very popular.

11

D DAY MINUS THREE

My transfer to the command ship offered me new interests and the opportunity to be with the top Commanders; some were friends of mine. It was D minus three days. The next two days were quiet and boring with little more than the sound and movement of the sea to attract our interest; however, on D minus one, things began to happen.

Mid-afternoon, about fifty miles off the island of Saipan, our convoy of 500 ships stopped dead in the water to make a shift of personnel. The mirrored waters were ghostly calm without so much as a ripple. It seemed as though someone had ordered this condition to ease the problem of the transfers. I had read about the phenomenon of mirror-like seas but had never experienced it. This was the "day the waters stood still."

During the early evening of D minus one day, a Japanese prisoner was brought aboard our ship. He was a survivor from a ship which our Naval Forces had sunk when it attempted to flee the Saipan harbor. When I first saw him, he was on the deck being questioned by men from our Intelligence section and was squealing like a pig. When he realized that he was not going to be dismembered, he calmed down and became very cooperative. When I approached him I noticed he had slick, oily skin and smelled strongly of fish. I was told this was a direct result of a diet which consisted mainly of fish. He was given food by a black steward, and I later overheard this steward tell his buddies with a giggle, "He saluted me!"

One of the characteristics of the Japanese soldier was great discipline and quick reaction to commands. The word "capture" was not in their training so they followed commands from their captors without discrimination.

We had another young Japanese from Saipan aboard our ship who had been captured during a previous operation, and true to form, he was personable and willing to cooperate with us. He was brought along because his knowledge of the Saipan terrain would be of value to us. Many prisoners taken early on Saipan were completely cooperative the day after their capture, and some were used to lead our Rangers to ammunition dumps and other sensitive targets in rear areas.

12

D DAY SAIPAN

Nobody slept after our breakfast of steak and eggs, and many of us watched as dawn slowly came over the horizon making the outline of the mountains visible. Our command ship had moved out front and was headed very slowly for the landing beach. The convoy was now deployed; the command ship led the formation followed by landing ships, personnel carriers, supply ships, and destroyers. The aircraft carriers were positioned just over the horizon where they had the much needed room to launch and land their planes. The battleships were now located on our flanks. As we drew nearer the beach the day grew lighter allowing me to see sugar mills to the right and left of center and the buildings of Chalan Kanoa, the capitol city. The town of Garapan was about three miles to our left. To our far left I could see Japanese freighters moving near Tanapag Harbor. The Navy preferred not to sink any of these freighters for fear they might block the harbor from our use.

Everything looked very peaceful, not at all like a war zone. I could see our battleships slowly maneuvering at a distance on our flanks. To our rear, the landing crafts were being launched by the hundreds as they were dispatched to the various ships to receive troops. These crafts, after being loaded, lined up in waves some distance offshore. At the appointed time they began their movement to shore. Tanks that were modified to negotiate the reefs led the way. Some of them were dispatched a short distance from shore because of the reef.

The battleships had maintained their interdiction fire throughout the night, and at daybreak wave after wave of carrier-based bombers flew over concentrating their fire along our landing area.

• An Eyewitness Account •

As our command ship moved closer to shore, the landing crafts overtook us. For the last few hundred yards, all weapons available on the landing crafts were continuously fired. The air in front of us soon became a blanket of tracer bullets and deafening noise. There was so much fire directed at the shore that it was impossible to detect any answering fire coming our way from the Japanese. The antiaircraft bursts fired against our dive-bombers were so inaccurate that, throughout the entire landing, I saw only one of our planes go down.

During the landing our ship pulled up within a few hundred yards of the beach and anchored. From this position, we had a front row seat to the most awesome conflict ever contrived by man. The concentration of fire power in this small area was the greatest ever employed in the history of warfare.

By the time our men hit the beaches, artillery counterfire became evident. Shell bursts made the beach appear like the sand was boiling. Occasionally, the Japanese would spray a few shots at our command ship with their heavy machine guns just to let us know they were there.

Because we were anchored so close to the beach, our facilities were to be used to care for the most severe casualties, and the wounded began to come aboard within minutes of the landing. Among the first casualties to come aboard was a young Marine with what appeared to be a shoulder shot off. I can still see his young shock-frozen face, the first of many. It was soon impossible to evacuate all the casualties. Casualties were brought aboard so fast, they had to be lined up on the deck. The beach was covered with men who were either dead or dying. Many of the wounded were hit again before they could be evacuated from the beach.

We continued to receive artillery fire until our men could neutralize the Japanese units. Later in the day, after we had achieved stability in the landing area, we began to receive fire from a large artillery gun located on Tinian Island. From our position, the island lay to the right and to our rear a distance of about one mile. Before this gun was silenced, it had caused some damage to the Battleship *Tennessee*. The harassment from Tinian continued for several days with no further damage to any of our ships.

By the end of the first day the beachhead was somewhat secure, and the Japanese had been pushed back for a few hundred feet. They did not commit their infantry on the beaches but relied instead on heavy machine guns, artillery, and tanks for their initial defense. Their defense was far more stubborn than anticipated, and by the end of the second day, our forces had not yet reached the first day's objectives. It was at this point the central Command Post was moved from ship to shore, and I went ashore with personnel of the antiaircraft command.

We climbed down the side of the ship with the aid of rope ladders to board the landing crafts. The descent was not difficult, but it was necessary to time our release from the rope with the rise and fall of the craft due to waves bobbing it up and down. Once we were aboard the landing craft, it was a short trip to the beach. We had to wade ashore from the reef holding our rifles, side arms, and ammunition over our heads.

The beach was littered for miles with disabled vehicles of every description. It looked like a junk yard. Hundreds of young Marines lined the beaches looking very much like sun bathers, but all were dead. Many of them had been stripped of most of their clothing by the medics in an attempt to treat their wound. The horror of death was familiar and expected, but there was little time to dwell on any of it. The wounded and maimed were our main concern.

The command center was set up in a residence on the main street of Chalan Kanoa. The building occupied by the antiaircraft Headquarters was a semi-open masonry type building. Most of the flooring was dirt, yet the house was very neat. Each person dug his own foxhole in the front yard of the house. These foxholes were used only once which was late that evening when two Japanese planes flew over us. Regular antiaircraft guns were not yet ashore, but individual rifle fire was immediately directed against the invading planes. I was pressed as low as I could possibly get in my foxhole and looked up to see the planes fly very low over me. I could also see the rifle fire ricocheting off them.

Once we heard the clanging noise of several tanks nearby. They appeared to be moving back and forth along our line of contact. The clap of the motors and distinctive clangor of metal made me believe they were Japanese. In the starlight, I could see General H. M. Smith, the force commander, nervously moving about his position which reinforced my fears that the situation was grave. This was confirmed the next morning by the ground forces around us. They reported the Japanese had tried unsuccessfully for a counterattack in our area. Some Japanese soldiers attempted to infiltrate back into our area, while many of them sought cover, making no attempt to catch up with their retreating units. Once separated from their units, they became more or less harmless. Many of them hid for days without being detected.

The third day we moved the Army Antiaircraft Artillery headquarters to a ridge located about one half mile inland. We set up camp in a Japanese farm house where it was evident that the family had hastily moved prior to our invasion, as there were toys and dolls still lying around.

As we moved up to this area, we saw the carnage from the previous day's action. Our own dead had been removed, but there had not been sufficient time to remove the Japanese soldiers. There was occasionally a body which had been run over by vehicles so many times it was difficult to recognize it as ever having been a body. By this time, the stench was terrible. As the bodies deteriorated, the swelling caused their arms to extend up and outwardly, as if they were so many stuffed dolls. My attitude toward them was one of curiosity and vengeance.

• The POA Defense •

Our second night on the island was worse than the first. We were in an area of several man-made caves, and we were not sure whether or not they contained Japanese troops. We also found the former site of the Japanese artillery unit which had shelled the landing forces on the beach.

The first line of the Japanese defense was concentrated in the general area of the beach. After breaking through this line, their defense became weaker enabling our forces to move forward at a faster pace. At the same time, however, our area of occupation was multiplied many times, and weak spots developed. We had learned from previous operations that it was possible to pass over many Japanese soldiers without detecting them in this larger area. They were experts in concealment, and on some occasions they went for several days in our location before being detected. We were aware of this danger and decided it would be safer to spend the night in our foxholes rather than in the house. The foxholes had been dug in an organized pattern for mutual security, and since we were in close proximity of the enemy, there was no noise or movement during the night. Consequently, we could not huddle together for a feeling of mutual support. Spread out as we were, we felt very alone in the midst of the enemy which made for a long, anxious night.

The next morning it was determined that the caves did contain Japanese. We made an effort to persuade them to come out by using their own people as spokesmen, but not one person came out. As a last resort, our bulldozers closed the entrances entombing them.

It had been determined from past experience that the bulldozer and flame thrower were the best weapons to use against their practice of digging in and refusing to come out. While the bulldozers were there, we had them push the dead Japanese soldiers and farm animals into a large bomb crater and cover them up. The stench had become unbearable.

• An Eyewitness Account •

At this point we moved a short distance up the hill and set up our station in a coconut palm grove. Part of our bivouac extended a short distance into a cane field, which had been the site of a Japanese artillery unit. This was the unit that placed fire on the beach directly in front of the Command ship. The guns had been emplaced in interconnecting trenches and cleverly camouflaged.

Once we were in place, the mobile kitchen went into operation and with a little imagination did a fair job in feeding us. The cooks augmented our regular rations of concentrated food bars with items taken from a large Japanese storehouse. These items, among other things, contained canned crab meat, canned mandarin oranges, rice, and the famous Japanese rice wine called Sake. They even suprised us once with a rice pudding.

From our new position, we had a commanding view of Aslito Airfield, the ocean area, the southern portion of the Island of Saipan, and the northern part of the Island of Tinian; this was an ideal site for our semi-permanent headquarters. I had a canvas folding cot and a tent for shelter which gave me a bit of comfort. But because of the rotting human and animal remains in the area, we had an explosion in the population of flies. Any time we used the latrine, we were attacked by squadrons of pests. As flies became a major hazard for our troops, the island was eventually sprayed from the air with DDT.

Except for the noise of the incessant firing from artillery and the occasional stray bullets in camp, we managed to be relatively comfortable during the day. Nightfall brought its own set of problems. Sleep was constantly interrupted by harassment fire, and even though we craved rest, we had to forego this luxury and leap for our foxholes. My back was already sore, and the clods of dirt seemed to get harder and harder every time I had to dive for cover.

As time passed, we got used to the gunfire and some of the fear vanished. In some respects, we feared the fire from our own

Figure 38. Saipan June 15, 1944. LST beached on coral reef after discharge of attack personnel and armament.

Figure 39. Saipan, June, 1944. Replacement troops wading ashore from beached LSTs.

Figure 40. Saipan, June, 1944. Amplifiers set up to broadcast instructions to civilians and military who may or may not be in our custody.

Figure 41. Marines pinned down on landing Iwo Jima beach.

Figure 42. Iwo Jima, February 1945. Portable flame thrower in action.

Figure 43. Aftermath of Iwo Jima assault February 19, 1945.

UNITED STATES PACIFIC FLEET
AND PACIFIC OCEAN AREAS
Headquarters of the Commander in Chief

Serial 000147

21 November 1944

From: Commander in Chief, Pacific Ocean Areas.
To :   Commander, Fifth Fleet
          Commanding General, U. S. Army Forces,
            Pacific Ocean Areas.
          Commanding General, U. S. Army Air Forces,
            Pacific Ocean Areas.
          Commander Amphibious Forces, Pacific Fleet,
          Commanding General, Tenth Army.
          Commander Forward Area, Central Pacific.

Subject: Command Relationships in the Ryukyus Operation.

Reference: (a) CinCPOA secret serial 0080 of 16 August
              1944.

     1.   The operations which involve the establishment of
the forces of the Pacific Ocean Areas in the Ryukyus differ from the
previous operations in the Central Pacific campaign in that, although
initially they will be amphibious in nature, they will involve the use
of a Field Army in one or more large islands for a considerable period.
Also the positions to be occupied are so close to major enemy bases
that active combat conditions will continue for an extended period.
The command relationships required will differ from those heretofore
prescribed for operations for the purpose of capture and occupation of
small island positions remote from Japan. The provisions of reference
(a) are, for planning purposes in connection with the Ryukyus operation,
modified as set forth in the following paragraphs.

     2.   The Commanding General, TENTH Army, will when
directed command the forces assigned to the Ryukyus. He will be
responsible for the development and defense of the island positions
involved and for the sea areas within twenty-five miles hereof.
The garrisons in the Ryukyus, together with such troops, shore-
based tactical air forces, and local naval defense forces as may
be assigned thereto, will constitute a joint task force, of which
the Commanding General, TENTH Army, will be the Task Force Commander.
He will normally be responsible directly to the Commander in Chief,
Pacific Ocean Areas, but may be placed under the command of a Task
Fleet Commander when the situation so requires.

UNCLASSIFIED   - 1 -

Figures 44-46. Letter of instructions from Admiral Chester W. Nimitz to area commanders.

Subject: Command Relationships in the Ryukyus Operation.

- -

3.   The responsibility for the sea areas to the northward
and westward of the Forward Area, Central Pacific will rest with the
Commander in Chief, Pacific Ocean Areas, except when delegated to a Task
Fleet Commander. The northern and western boundaries of the Forward
Area, Central Pacific will be announced separately.

4.   The Commanding General, TENTH Army will initially
have the status of Commanding General, Expeditionary Troops, as set forth
in reference (a). When the officer commanding the Operation (Commander,
FIFTH Fleet) has determined that the amphibious phase of the operations at
each objective has been completed he will direct that command of all
forces on shore at that objective pass to the Commanding General, TENTH
Army, whereupon the latter will assume responsibility to him for the defense
and development of positions captured. The organization and administration
of the area and of the defense forces assigned will then conform to directives
issued by the Commander in Chief, Pacific Ocean Areas, to the Commanding
General, TENTH Army.

5.   When the situation permits, the Commander in Chief,
Pacific Ocean Areas will relieve the Officer Commanding the Operation
(Commander, FIFTH Fleet) of the responsibility for the defense and
development of the Ryukyus. Thereafter, the Commanding General, TENTH
Army, will be responsible direct to the Commander in Chief, Pacific Ocean
Areas.

6.   It is intended to assign a general officer of the Army
Ground Forces as Island Commander, Okinawa, to exercise command of the
garrison of the island (including Ie Shima), and to conduct its development
and defense under the direction of the Commanding General, TENTH Army.
The naval operating base and naval air bases at Okinawa will be included
in the island command. It is intended to constitute the air forces
assigned to the Ryukyus as a joint air task force, under a general officer
of the Marine Corps to be designated the Tactical Air Force, Ryukyus, with
its commander responsible direct to the Commanding General, TENTH Army.
Strategic air forces and naval search squadrons based in the Ryukyus will,
however, normally be assigned to the operational control of the Commanding
General, Army Air Forces, POA and Commander Fifth Fleet respectively.
The naval local defense forces in the Ryukyus will constitute a task force
commanded by a flag officer of the Navy responsible to the Commanding
General, TENTH Army.

- 2 -

UNCLASSIFIED

Subject: Command Relationships in the Ryukyus Operation.

- -

      7.   In the preparation of plans for combat operations during the amphibious phase, the Commanding General, TENTH Army will deal directly with the Commander Joint Expeditionary Force (Commander Amphibious Force, Pacific Fleet). In the preparation of plans for subsequent operations, and for the development and defense of the area, he will deal directly with the Commander in Chief, Pacific Ocean Areas, and with the Administrative and Type Commanders of all services as necessary.

      8.   At such time as it may become necessary to assign the Commanding General, TENTH Army, to conduct offensive operations outside the Ryukyus the provisions of this directive will be amended in the light of the circumstances then existing.

                                          C. W. NIMITZ

Copy to:

      Cominch

    O. L. Thorne,
Flag Secretary.

Headquarters United States Army Forces, Pacific Ocean Areas

Inter-Staff Routing Slip

For use in all inter-office correspondence. Separate each Memorandum
by a line and initial. *Memorandum will preferably be typewritten.*

SUBJECT: Commendation by the Commander-in-Chief.

Memo. No.	Date	From	To	Memorandum
1	30 NOV 1944	ArtyO	C/S CG	1. I believe that the Commanding General would be interested in seeing the attached commendation from General MacArthur on the superior performance of our antiaircraft units on Leyte. 2. The Pacific Ocean Areas antiaircraft units involved are: Hq & Hq Btry, 97th AA Group 502d AAA Gun Battalion 504th AAA Gun Battalion 485th AAA AW Battalion 861st AAA AW Battalion 866th AAA AW Battalion Elements of the 294th, 295th, and 230th Slt Bns. 3. Please return. H. B. HOLMES, JR., Brig. Gen., USA. 1 Incl: Cy of ltr of Commendation.

EJM/tdg - 201.22/3

| 2 | 1 Dec 1944 | Arty | ArtyO | NOTED BY COMGENPOA

JOSEPH R. GROVES
Lieutenant Colonel, GSC,
ADC of S. |

Figures 47-50. Letter of commendation to AAA units 97th AAA Group.

AG 201.22   1st Ind
  (4Nov 44)
HEADQUARTERS SIXTH ARMY, APO 442, 6 November 1944.

To: Commanding General, 32d AAA Brigade, APO 72.

      I am pleased to note this commendation and wish to add my appre-
ciation of the splendid performance of antiaircraft artillery units
participating in th Leyte operation.

                              /s/ Walter Krueger
                              /t/ WALTER KRUEGER,
                              Lieutenant General, U. S. Army,
                                      Commanding.

201.22   2d Ind.   HC/ph
Headquarters, 32d AAA Brigade, APO 72, 16 November 1944.

To: Group, battalion and battery commanders.

      1. I am delighted to transmit these commendations.

      2. The credit for destroying so many Japanese planes and for turning
back almost all of the rest goes almost entirely to the men and officers
in firing batteries and sections and I wish to express my appreciation of
their alertness and skill in delivering fire against every possible target.

                              /s/ Homer Case,
                              /t/ HOMER CASE,
                              Brigadier General, U.S. Army,
                                      Commanding.

A CERTIFIED TRUE COPY:

Rodman A Garren
RODMAN A. GARREN
1st Lt., CAC
Adjutant

35308

4 November 1944

SUBJECT: Commendation by the Commander-in-Chief:

THRU : Commanding General, Sixth Army

TO   : Brig. General Homer Case, Commanding 32nd AA Brigade.

1. General MacArthur has directed that the antiaircraft artillery organizations of SWPA and of POA participating in the air defenses of of Leyte be informed of his admiration for the high standard of technical performance manifested by the antiaircraft troops up to date.

2. When informed of the total number of hostile planes destroyed, probably destroyed or damaged by antiaircraft fire, he commented, "This is superior shooting."

3. I add my compliments to the troops of the antiaircraft defenses for the splendid record established thus far against hostile airplane attacks under most trying circumstances.

                                        /s/ W. F. Marquat
                                        /t/ W. F. MARQUAT
                                        Major General, U.S.A.

A CERTIFIED TRUE COPY:

RODMAN A. GARREN
1st Lt., CAC
Adjutant

35308   - 1 -

*Reference AAA Troops We
diverted to McArthur for
his drive on the Phillipines
WCS*

22 November 1944

Lt. Col., William C. Smith, CAC,
Area Artillery Officer,
Hqs. USAF Pacific Ocean Areas,
APO #958.

Dear Smith:

    1. Thanks for the pat on the back. I admit with a modest blush
that the mounting scoreboard of the outfit (and the pile of empty brass)
entitles us to a file in "A" Company of the world's AAA regiments. I am
enclosing General MacArthur's comment. We are still sharpening our claws
for more game.

    2. Due to announced SWPA policy I regret that I cannot give you
one man's opinions without clearing through GHQ. If you can take the delay
I would be glad to do so if you will apply to C.G. SWPA. However, I think
a few comments are permissable as information rather than opinion.

        a. I have the greatest confidence in the breadth and soundness
of the opinions of the observer from the Buckner Boys, Major Crane, who
must be available to you, and who cussed and discussed the operation at
length with me, my staff and on down the chain of command. I have not seen
his report, but I will guarantee it is worth reading.

        b. Crane can tell you what new wrinkles we advocate in search-
lights. All I can say is that my concept of the role as I presented it
to General Holmes just before I left has not changed.

        c. At about A / 20 I reread your report on Forager. In the
light of fresh experience I saw so much more in it that it was like reading
a new document. It is a fine piece of work and, except for minor details,
I concur heartily in the findings and recommendations.

    3. · Please give my kindest regards to General Holmes, and tell him
that I am sorrier than ever that I could not take him up on the equipment
proffered just before we left. I would appreciate it too, if you would tell
Hendon of the Searchlights that you heard from me.

            Come out and see me sometime.

                                            L. L. CLAYTON
                                            Colonel, CAC
1 Incl: Commanding
    Ltr 14 AA Command

20 November 1944.

Lt Col Wm. C. Smith, C.A.C.,
Area Artillery Office, POA,
APO 958.

Dear Smith,

      Received both your letters of the 11th, one brought by Comdr Walker and the other reference employment of searchlights. Walker is, as you mentioned, very cooperative and a fine person to work with. He has had considerable trouble in getting located, and may have to set up at a temporary site and move later to the permanent location when service roads and facilities are extended to include that area. I have helped him as much as I could, but, as you know, there is no construction that has a priority less than urgent.

      Reference the use of searchlights I must admit that the situation is still obscure. First of all, I will answer your questions, in order:

      Recent targets over Saipan were not illuminated. Searchlights at Tinian were in action but lights on this island were kept out of action. The only use of searchlights here for illumination has been to establish identity of planes presumably friendly but with IFF not showing.

      As a result of the raids, an additional automatic weapons battery was moved to Isley Field from the ammunition storage area at Marpi Point. Searchlights in the Isley Field area have been fitted with spread beam attachments and a plan is being studied for increasing the number of lights at Isley and fitting these lights with spread beam attachments for illumination of low-flying aircraft.

      No attempts were made to illuminate low-flying aircraft. The Japs have confined their raids to moonlit nights, and automatic weapons have been able to engage planes without additional illumination.

      Lights are being equipped with spread beam attachment, ~~borrowed from seacoast units~~; it is planned to put in spare lights, sited to obtain illumination of hostile aircraft attacking at low elevations. How successful these lights will be I don't know, but the ability of the gun batteries to attack and destroy hostile planes without illuminating them indicates the most practical use of the lights will probably be in support of automatic weapons fire.

Figure 51-52. Letter dated 20 November, 1944 from HQ Garrison Force, Saipan.

There are so many new plans being made for the defense of the principal airfields that they will possibly cause some mutual interference. It is proposed, for example, to set up all spare cal. .50 machine guns of Air Force units and site them for barrage fire in certain critical sectors, all banks of guns being fired electrically. Request has further been made by Air Force units to apply passive measures of defense, present proposal being to blanket the field with smoke in event of a raid. It is evident that the use of smoke and automatic weapons are mutually exclusive, but we are getting ready to make tests to see how it will work out. If anything interesting develops, I will let you know.

Things are going along pretty well out here. We are all busy and glad to be. Our CP is now located on the hill overlooking Tanapag Harbor and we find the weather much nicer. The AAA Hq has a fine location and a well developed area at Hill 500. We have no complaints except that I still believe I was right about the 120mm guns. One of these days someone will be wanting to lift our 155mm batteries, and where will we be should an attack take place? I'm not as worried about it here as much as they were worrying about the defense of Oahu when I left, but the situation could be embarrassing.

Thank you for your letters. If I can further obscure the situation, let me know.

With best wishes,

CHARLES B. DUFF
Lt Col, C. A.

THE BROADCASTER

PUBLISHED BY THE STUDENTS OF WHITEHAVEN SCHOOL

WHITEHAVEN, TENNESSEE, APRIL, 1944

OUR SMITH FAMILY GOES TO WAR

Major Wm. C. Smith   **Sgt. Wade T. Smith**   **First Lieut. Russell L. Smith**   **Sgt. Eulyse Smith**   **Pfc. Eugene C. Smith**

Pictured above are five sons of Mr. and Mrs. W. B. Smith who are now in various branches of the armed service. They appear according to their ages, ranging from oldest to youngest, left to right. Four of these five brothers are graduates of Whitehaven School.

Major William C. Smith, known to his friends as Bill, is now stationed in the Hawaiian Islands where he is Assistant Chief of Staff of the Hawaiian Coast Artillery. He has been on duty in Hawaii since the summer of 1941.

Bill finished high school in Ripley, Miss., in 1928 just is now stationed in the Hawaiian Islands where he is Assistant Chief of Staff of the Hawaiian Coast Artillery. He has been on duty in Hawaii since the summer of 1941.

Bill finished high school in Ripley, Miss., in 1928 just before his family moved to Whitehaven. He then attended Mississippi State College from which he was graduated with a major in electrical engineering. He was stationed at Schofield Barracks at Pearl Harbor at the time of the Japanese attack on December 7, 1941. While visiting his parents last summer, he told many interesting stories of the raid and the weeks that followed. One of the most interesting stories of these days was an account of his taking some of his men into a Japanese village adjoining his barracks and seizing $10,000 worth of the finest radio equipment to be found in the world. The Japanese, who picked pineapples for $5 a week, were all taken into custody. Since this time Major Smith has made tours of most of the Middle Pacific Islands and helped settle the island which was the first stepping stone in taking the Gilbert Islands.

Sgt. Wade T. Smith is now stationed at Fort Benning, Ga., with the Seventh Armored Division, having enlisted in 1942. He is connected with the parts department. Wade graduated from Whitehaven High School in 1933. He entered the University of Tennessee a year later, majoring in business administration. In high school he was a valued member of the Glee Club and was a member of the first Show Club.

First Lieut. Russell L. Smith is now an Operations Officer with the Army Air Corps somewhere in the South Pacific. He went overseas in November, 1943, and was located in New Guinea for a short while. He recently moved to another scene of action. He reports that he had lost several nights' sleep and keeps pretty busy.

Russell finished Whitehaven school with the class of 1935. He entered the University of Tennessee the following fall and majored in business administration, graduating in June, 1939. While a student in the university he was especially interested in military training and took all the higher military courses offered. He joined the Army immediately after his graduation and was located in Fort Lewis, Wash., for two years.

Sgt. Eulyse M. Smith is a Base Technical Inspector at the Smyrna Air Base at Smyrna, Tenn. His duties range from checking technical order files and Army regulations to Liberator bombers. In addition to his regular duties he has been helping his buddies with their legal problems and giving assistance to the civilians on the Post with their income tax problems. He writes, "In all, my work is most interesting and I really enjoy every bit of it, but like others, I am looking forward to the day when we shall again take up the real American way of life—that of peaceful pursuits."

Eulyse finished Whitehaven High School in 1937. In his senior year he played an outstanding role in the first of the Shakespearean plays inaugurated by the Speech Department under the direction of Mr. Eugene Bence. In the same year he won the State Oratorical Contest in the High School Inter-Scholastic League held in Knoxville. Following his graduation from high school, Eulyse entered Memphis State College. After two years of study there he transferred to the University of Texas and worked his way through the law school. After his admittance to the bar, he entered the service in May, 1942, and spent

five months at Sheppard Field awaiting call to Cadet School. Last May he had to give up the idea of flying when he struck acrobatics in primary flight training because of air sickness. Since that time he has been stationed at the four-engine transition school for pilots at Smyrna.

Pfc. Eugene Smith graduated in Whitehaven's class of 1942 and entered Memphis State that fall. He completed three quarters in college and went into the Army. He took basic training at Miami, then went to mechanics school at Amarillo, Texas. He was then transferred to of 1942 and entered Memphis State that fall. He completed three quarters in college and went into the Army. He took basic training at Miami, then went to mechanics school at Amarillo, Texas. He was then transferred to Scott Field, Ill., for further training in airplane propellers. He graduated and is now an Airplane Propeller Specialist and at the present is in Kearns, Utah, awaiting overseas shipment. Gene is the youngest member of the Smith family.

Another brother, Clarence Smith, is employed in the War Department in Washington, D. C. Guy Smith, the oldest of the seven brothers, is also engaged in an essential occupation. He is a dairy farmer on the Smith Farm near Germantown. A sister, Mrs. Beatrice Smith Hinkel, also a graduate of Whitehaven, who lives in Washington, D. C., spends much of her time as a nurse's aid in a Washington hospital. Besides the four sons mentioned above and Mrs. Hinkel two other members of the family graduated from Whitehaven School, Mrs. Callie Smith Hatton and Mrs. Margaret Smith Bence.

Whitehaven School is happy to have had Mr. and Mrs. Smith as patrons for a period of 14 years. All of their family of seven sons and seven daughters finished high school; seven of them graduated from Ripley High School in Mississippi and seven from Whitehaven High School. A good percentage of them has graduated from colleges, universities, and business schools. The school will follow with a great deal of pride and interest their five sons in the service.

Personality Talks
Sponsored By Club

The open house at the Triple S Lounge on March 10 was a huge success.

On March 13, Miss Peggy Kelly from Southwestern talked on "The Psychology of Love." Mrs. E. V. Zumwalt talked on March 20 and 28 about "Conversation and Voice Control" and "Public Speaking and Story Telnig." "Parlor Tricks" was the subject on April 3. Mrs. Newton Stern reviewed a book on April 10. On April 17 and 24 the topics will be "Dating from a Boy's Point of View" and "Dating From a Girl's Point of View. "Do's and Don'ts" will be the subject on May 1. Mrs. Lucian Dent will talk on "Hobbies." "Clothes and How to Wear Them" will be the theme of the lecture on May 15.

"Art Appreciation" and "Music Appreciation" are to be discussed

THEY PLAY ON A GREATER STAGE

Winifred Scarborough, P. O. 2/c   **Cpl. Ernest Wilson**   **Cpl. William G. Phelps**

In September, 1936, among the large group of p[...]oted to this position and his success as an in-

Beta Club Sponsors
Memphis Convention

The Whitehaven Chapter of the Beta Club sponsored the first West Tennessee Convention, which was held at the Peabody Hotel on April 14.

Miss Hannah Leitner from the National office attended. About 160 students attended also.

The day's program included a morning session at which reports were given from different committees from the various chapters. After the reports the members were addressed by several speakers.

Next on the program was a luncheon. Since April 14 was Pan-American Day, this was featured at the luncheon. Also at the luncheon there were several musical numbers by members of the various chapters.

During the afternoon commit-

Figure 54. Typical cave in Saipan.

Figure 55. Block house on Garapan beach now being used to store sail surfing equipment.

Figure 56. Col. Smith at the site of the Banzai attack near Tanapag, Saipan.

Figure 57. Site of Japanese prison where downed American airmen were imprisoned on Saipan.

Figure 58. Suicide Cliff at Lagua Katan Point.

Figure 59. Col. Smith at grave side of guide's sister killed by Naval gunfire during the battle for Saipan.

Figure 60. Guide points out to Col. Smith Disabled Tank on Red Beach, Saipan.

Figure 61. Col. Smith and his wife, Frances, on Blue Beach, Saipan, where he came ashore with the Marines, June 16, 1944.

troops more than that from the enemy. Fresh troops on their first night ashore shot at anything that moved, a fact which soon annihilated the farm animal population. This situation grew so bad that we actually reviewed the possibility of requiring first-nighters to remove their ammunition from their rifles, but no action was ever taken.

On our second day ashore many of our naval warships and supply vessels began to move back out to sea because of the threat the Japanese fleet still presented to our battle force. When the two fleets finally did meet in combat the confrontation became known as the battle of the Philippine Sea. Had our Navy lost this battle and our supplies, we would have been at the mercy of the Japanese fleet.

The Japanese had planned this encounter with our Navy for several weeks and hoped for a major victory. They vowed to stop us at any cost, and this battle was to strike the fatal blow. The tide of battle was so much in our favor that the Navy called it the Great Marianas Turkey Shoot. Most of this action occurred on June 19, 1944. The Japanese lost four hundred planes and three aircraft carriers while the United States losses numbered fifty-eight aircraft and the Battleship *South Dakota*. After this encounter, the Japanese Fleet was never again a viable force. We captured many ships in this action, one of which was a carrier that took part in the Pearl Harbor attack. I was especially elated over this bit of news.

The struggle for Saipan was a difficult fight, and we suffered many casualties in wounded and dead. The Army division did not participate in the original assault, but came ashore two days later on the most southern beach area under the command of Major General Ralph Smith. On more than one occasion, he had dined with us at the Burgin Manor and was a respected acquaintance. His original assignment was an area which included Aslito Airfield and the southeast portion of Saipan. One portion of this area, on Natufan Point, was very rugged with huge rocks, scrub growth, concrete pillboxes, and Japanese soldiers.

The Japanese had fortified this area with extra defense barriers as they expected it would be the point of our initial landing. This build up and the natural rocky terrain made our artillery and mortar fire ineffective, thereby slowing the advancement of General Smith's forces. At this point Marine General Holland M. Smith became impatient with the delay and ordered the Army Commander to speed up his advance. General Ralph Smith was reluctant to shove his men into a certain deathtrap preferring instead to advance in a slow, careful manner.

The strategy of the Marine Corps is, for the most part, to slug it out in a frontal assault, taking advantage of shock. The Army, on the other hand, depends more on flanking maneuvers and piecemeal annihilation of the enemy. There is a need for both tactics as each has its advantages and disadvantages. For point targets, such as small islands, there is no room to maneuver, leaving little choice other than a head-on attack. The Marines were masters of this. Saipan was our first land mass large enough to have a choice in the type of attack used, and we used both.

Hostility had been building between the two generals since the battle for Kwajalein. At that time the Army commander had complained to General Holland M. Smith that his Marines were moving forward too fast, leaving behind their lines many entrenched Japanese. The Army commander claimed that this haste required his troops to clean up the sector behind the Marines. This new dispute caused the Marine commander to remove Army General Ralph Smith from his command. General Ralph Smith was recognized by his peers as a superior officer, and this incident was not considered a blight on his record. Nevertheless, the removal of General Smith was probably the most serious threat to Marine-Army relations in the entire war.

The staff at Army Antiaircraft Artillery headquarters was aware of the problem the army units were having in their advance and offered assistance from our ninety and twenty millimeter antiaircraft guns. For the first time, our guns were using proximity fuses on the ninety millimeter shells. This fuse caused the shell to burst when it neared the target, thus spraying shrapnel from above. The overhead bursts were more effective than the regular artillery ground bursts against the protection of the boulders. Also twenty millimeter automatic guns proved to be very effective for shooting into the caves. Although the rifle and hand grenades were more lethal than the twenty millimeter explosive shells, their rapid fire and long range made them a weapon to be reckoned with.

Credit from the infantry battalion commander was given to the AAA for killing between two and three hundred of the approximately eight hundred enemy casualties found in the area. The shelling also shredded the scrubby growth on the rocky terrain making the job of the infantry easier.

The Army Antiaircraft Artillery headquarters was routinely furnished with a situation map showing the position of our troops. The latest map showed our front lines had reached a position where, according to my preliminary design, an AAA gun battery was to be situated. I was anxious to see if my aerial map study checked out with the actual conditions, so the commander and I decided to take a look at the area.

We drove to the spot and got out of the jeep to walk over the area. It seemed very quiet and we both agreed that the site was perfect for our gun battery. I was patting myself on the back for my selection when a Marine stepped out from his concealment. In a typical calm, war-weary, stolid manner, he informed us the enemy occupied the low hill a short distance away and that we were in an unsafe area. We quickly turned on our heels and headed for the jeep just as bursts from knee mortars began popping around us. Our exit from the area was somewhat like the Lone Ranger when he leaped on his horse and galloped after the bad guys. The Japanese could have easily picked us off with their rifles, but that would have revealed their exact location, whereas the mortar fire was coming from a safe distance behind their front line defenders.

As areas were occupied, we were faced with the problem of how to handle the civilians. As soon as possible, they were all collected and moved to a central location where they were screened and organized into groups. Leaders of these groups were selected from their own people, sometimes with unexpected results. I recall one instance when a sugar cane worker was appointed leader of a group that put him in charge of the former manager of the plant where he had worked. He took great pleasure in the switch of authority and took advantage of every opportunity to reverse the tables.

The next morning our doctor was one of those dispatched to make sick call on the encampment. A young Japanese girl told him that during the night she had had sex with one of her fellow prisoners. She told him she wanted something to keep her from having a baby. The thought came to me that it takes more than confusion by the noise of battle and the carnage of war to stop the act of sex.

On many occasions the Japanese air force, which was operating out of Guam, dropped bombs nearby in the Aslito Airfield area. We always had advance warning and took cover in foxholes. The greatest fright I remember came during one of these attacks. I had just jumped into my foxhole and looked up in the darkness to see the outline of a man poised with his arm raised as if to throw a hand grenade. My instant reaction was to point my pistol at him prepared to shoot. Just before I pulled the trigger, I realized it was one of our majors who was in the act of pulling on a sweater before settling into his foxhole. To this day, I am haunted with the thought that I had almost killed an American soldier.

It wasn't long before we started to make an impact with our

antiaircraft guns, and I was elated with the effectiveness the guns had against enemy aircraft. The first airplane shot out of the skies came over at night and was so high we could not hear it. It was detected and tracked by radar. The first bursts from our guns were on target, and we rejoiced when the flaming aircraft fell to the ground. The front line commanders reported that this action boosted the morale of their troops as nothing else had.

The Japanese civilians were so frightened by our invasion that many thousands of them lost their lives unnecessarily. Some holed up in caves, and pleas by their own people to come out fell on deaf ears. On many occasions the entrance of these caves were sealed because we did not know the extent of the threat these concealed Japennese posed for our troops. The number of civilians buried alive was small and this entombment only occurred early in the invasion when we had little or no time to identify the occupants of the caves. Usually the caves were reopened as soon as possible.

Occasionally, young children were deserted by their parents and left behind. These children usually showed no fear of us. When two other officers and I approached several children playing in a cane field, they made no move to retreat. In fact, they moved to meet us in order to satisfy their curiosity and got a good look, both front and rear. I wrote a letter home about this incident, but instead of telling it like it happened, I converted it to fiction with all the suspense I could build into it. I was disturbed and remorseful when I learned that as my mother read this letter she began screaming with horror and was unable to read the conclusion of the letter which revealed the way it actually happened.

In about two weeks the battle for the island was near completion, and I decided it was time for me to return to headquarters in Hawaii. My assignment as observer was primarily one of reporting on things related to defense against aircraft, directly and indirectly, and it appeared to me that mopping up was all that remained of the action.

• An Eyewitness Account •

The banzai attack is unique to Japanese military strategy and is staged by the remnants of the force when all hope for victory is lost. It is a suicidal last effort to kill as many of their enemy as possible. The Japanese prepare themselves for this effort usually by consuming a great quantity of intoxicants and start the ritual with a cheer to the Emperor wishing him a long life. The commander of the force commits hari-kari and the march begins.

A few days after I left, the Japanese staged their final effort with a banzai attack near Tanapag Harbor in the northwest portion of the island. Japanese General Saito mustered this legendary final effort with the remnants of his forces numbering three thousand men. Armed with rusty rifles, crude knives, bayonets, clubs, and miscellaneous weapons, this horde of stampeding men overran our defenders, pushing many of them into the sea before counterattack could be organized. In the face of our machine guns and direct fire by artillery, the Japanese kept advancing, although they had to climb over their fallen comrades to do so.

After this incident I felt that perhaps I had left too soon, that in my great haste to leave Saipan there may have been a slight breach in my self-discipline. Self-discipline is a must for officers with the responsibility, trust, and latitude of my position.

The four-engine airplane I boarded for the flight to Hawaii was loaded with so many wounded soldiers, we had no room to move between the stretchers. One of the plane's engines was leaking oil, but this did not stop the flight or cause me any concern. In fact, after takeoff from Aslito Airfield, and when safely out of range of scattered Japanese soldiers, I breathed a sigh of relief giving no thought to either the crippled plane or the fear that we might not make it.

We were two days en route to Hickam Field on Oahu, Hawaii. Since I had gone so long without real sleep and was unable to relax enough to sleep on the plane, I assisted in tending to the wounded. One young man, who had multiple wounds, was very still. A stench of rotting blood and flesh hung over him. At times I

92

wondered if he might be dead; however, near morning, he roused to ask me in his rural south, Alabama lingo, "Is there a treen on this plane?" I was relieved and glad to find out that he was not only alive, but able to go to the toilet with my assistance. This young man, along with the rest of the wounded, was transferred to the hospital on Kwajalein Island, 1250 miles east of Saipan. After this brief stop I continued on to Honolulu.

The battle for Saipan was costly in lives and equipment. American casualties were approximately seventeen thousand with over thirty-four hundred dead or missing. The Japanese lost almost their entire garrison of thirty-two thousand men. Numbered among other losses were five hundred and fifty native Chamorro and thirty thousand Japanese civilians, most of whom committed suicide. Aided and abetted by Japanese military, the civilians climaxed this ritual in a mass suicide by leaping from a cliff at Lagua Katan Point, the most northern portion of the island. The practice was for the parents to supervise the deaths of their children, then follow with their own suicide. In some cases, Japanese soldiers were standing by to shoot those reluctant to make the plunge from the cliff. Eventually, the soldiers either committed hari-kari or made the banzai death march attack. The total loss of life on Saipan was about sixty-six thousand people plus another seventeen thousand wounded U.S. soldiers.

What price victory! In all our previous assault operations, the Japanese had also resisted to their death, but this was our first operation where Japanese civilians were involved. There seems to be no parallel in modern day history to this near-total slaughter (directly or indirectly) of defeated personnel.

As the war progressed and their plight became more dire, the Japanese resorted to suicidal attacks with their air force. Specially trained Kamikaze pilots would dive their bomb-laden craft into our ships. This was an almost can't miss tactic. Pilots required neither advanced flight training for proficiency, nor a sophisticated plane.

13

IWO JIMA

Following Saipan, Tinian, and Guam, came Iwo Jima. The occupation of Iwo Jima was planned and executed using the same tactics previously used on the other small islands.

From the beginning, our staff was leery of the advisability of occupying Iwo Jima. By this time in late 1944, the Navy and Air Force had attained a wide margin of superiority in the area, and we felt that Iwo Jima should be bypassed. There were other islands nearby that had little or no defensive capacity, and it was our opinion that the cost of taking Iwo Jima outweighed the benefits to be derived. Bypassing islands had already proven to be good strategy; a good example was Truk, the most heavily fortified island in the Pacific area.

Additional information was supplied to us by Navy frogmen, causing us even more concern about a landing on Iwo Jima. We were alarmed by their reports of a bastion-type defensive network consisting of caves and trenches the Japanese had carved out of the lava on the island. Also, there was evidence of bizarre barricades and a plan to set fire to the entire beach area. The fire was to be ignited by exploding fuel-filled drums placed strategically along the beach. For some reason unknown to us, this plan was never carried out. Nonetheless, we were alarmed by the projected heavy loss of life if we attempted to occupy Iwo Jima.

Based on our knowledge of the terrain, we knew the landing would be hazardous. Moreover we knew that the fortified beaches would cost a great many lives before a beachhead could be established. We wished very much that the operation would be aborted, but our responsibility was to put together the means to do the job, not decide whether or not to take the island. That decision belonged to the Joint Chiefs of Staff in Washington.

As history shows, we paid an inordinate price for Iwo Jima. My heart aches for those who lost their lives there, and to this day the sculpted flag raising memorial commemorating this event leaves me cold. That cold monument is unrealistic and unrelated to the bleeding, dying Marines who gave their lives in that campaign. The cock does not crow twice, and there are few, if any, olés in combat. It is a long way from the battlefield to the patriotic display back home. For those who fought for them, life and freedom have a special flavor the protected will never know.

There is no way I can rationalize this expenditure of lives. On this occasion, many of us wished General MacArthur had been our commander. We felt that under his command there would never have been an Iwo Jima; although he received his orders from the Joint Chiefs of Staff as we did, on occasion he purportedly ignored them to do things his way.

It was not that we condoned General MacArthur's insubordination nor were we critical of Admiral Nimitz's strict adherence to the chain of command. Nevertheless, we ferverently wished the Iwo Jima mission had been aborted.

14

THE MOUNTAIN TOP—OKINAWA

The occupation of Okinawa in the Ryukyus island chain was a giant step forward, not only in geographic location but also in the size of the U.S. Forces used to assault the island. In some respects one might think of Okinawa as the mountain top overlooking the Promised Land.

This was the first time we were to use a force of Army size in our battle for the islands. The Tenth Army was formed for this purpose, and Major General Simon Bolivar Buckner was placed in command. In our initial assaults, the responsibilities of the Navy were so great that Admirals acted as the force commanders. At Saipan the tactics of ground warfare became much more complicated requiring a Marine general to be named as the force commander. The size of Okinawa meant a more open land style of warfare would be necessary, and as the Army adapts itself more to this type of maneuvering an Army general was the best choice for a Force Commander.

Army General Buckner was a descendent and namesake of the famous general of the Mexican and Civil War eras. He was my kind of man, and I came to know him very well while working with him in the formation of the antiaircraft artillery portion of the Tenth Army on Oahu. He wore the perpetual smile of an outgoing personality and was well-liked.

I was honored when the general asked me to join him as his chief of all artillery. This assignment meant an immediate promotion to full colonel. Most staff positions are not associated with rank, while some field positions carry automatic promotion to the rank prescribed for the assignment. I replied, "Thanks, but no thanks."

My reasons were simple. The war in Europe was nearing an end, and after Okinawa it appeared that there would be a complete reorganization of our command for the assault on the Japanese homeland. We looked upon this as the beginning of a new war with no relation to the island-hopping campaign we had been accustomed to. The emphasis would change from naval to land warfare where casualties would leap from thousands to hundreds of thousands. Should the Japanese defend their homeland with the same tenacity they had fought for their Pacific Islands, our casualties could very well run as high as five million dead.

We did not yet know about the existence of the atomic bomb or its tremendous strategic implications. It was our feeling that General MacArthur would rightly succeed Admiral Nimitz as supreme commander of the new organization. In that case many of us would be phased out in favor of men with whom he was accustomed to commanding in his southwest Pacific Area. In light of this, I decided it was time for me to rotate back to the mainland and made plans to do so. The forty-six month ordeal in the Pacific was taking its toll on me mentally and physically, another reason I reluctantly said "No" to the General. I felt I had fought the good fight and should go home on my own power rather than in a body bag. Everyone became eligible for transfer to the mainland after two years of service in the Pacific area. After qualifying, one could normally take advantage of this transfer at will. Previously, I had hesitated to rotate back lest I be sent to the European Theater.

My most coveted memory of General Buckner occurred at the Burgin Manor where we gave him a small *bon voyage* party just prior to his departure for the Okinawa assault. It was a relaxed, enjoyable evening and with each additional Old Fashion drink he consumed, his mouth opened wider and wider with laughter.

General Buckner lost his life early in the fight for Okinawa while visiting a forward artillery post. The chances are that had

• The POA Defense •

I accepted his invitation, I would have been by his side at the fateful moment, and only God knows if I would have survived. I can only say, "Rest in peace, my treasured friend."

15

ROTATION

I returned to the mainland as planned and landed May 7, 1945, at Tacoma, Washington on the eve of victory in Europe. I had asked the officer in charge of transportation to find me the slowest ship in the Pacific for my trip to the mainland as I very much desired a slack time free of responsibility. He almost overdid it. We were three weeks en route to Tacoma, Washington.

We sailed out of Honolulu harbor and had our first engine trouble off Diamond Head. After about one hour, we were underway again. At about one thousand miles out we had to stop for the better part of a day for repairs. We were sailing without escort, so we were a bit concerned about reports of an enemy submarine in our general area. Occasionally, Japanese submarines would ply the area in an attempt to harass shipping. On at least one occasion they surfaced and fired at one of our planes overhead.

I was the only passenger aboard this cargo ship, and for a while, the crew's attitude toward me was guarded. They wondered why I was aboard and decided that I must be along to check on them. I soon convinced them that my only purpose was to have a relaxing trip to the mainland. I decided to spend one day with each officer aboard and let him teach me his job. This turned out to be a big boost in the morale. Not only did I enjoy it, but this change in their routine was like a shot in the arm and put some enthusiasm back into their jobs. As a result they were no longer suspicious of me, and I was treated like a VIP.

It was an Army policy to give people with a long period of combat duty a chance for regionalizing. At the time I did not feel the need for this. However, I soon learned that it was needed by everyone, if for no other reason than orientation, and after a trip to a Miami Beach hotel for rehabilitation I was transferred to Fort Bliss, Texas. I was put in command of an antiaircraft artillery training regiment. This was June of 1945, a period I will never forget as this transfer put me under the light of the atomic bomb test at Alamorgardo, New Mexico on July 16, 1945.

When peace came, I accepted the first opportunity to withdraw from the service and was transferred back to the Reserves.

16

POST WAR

On December 7, 1971, I attended the Thirtieth Anniversary reunion of the Pearl Harbor Survivors' Association in Hawaii. While there I visited the site where I had seen the lead plane of the attack on Wheeler Field. The old buildings had been torn down, and a residential subdivision for American military families had been developed in the area. However, I brought along a prewar aerial photograph of the site, and with the aid of this photograph and some of the undisturbed landscape, I was able to pinpoint the exact spot where I stood as the attack began. When I located the area, without warning, I broke into convulsive crying. In all of my war experiences, I had never cried or even felt teary-eyed, but on this spot thirty years later I was crying like a baby.

Many people asked me, "How did you feel?" during some of the most distressing experiences of the war. For the answer to this I can only say that usually my experience was one of "non-feeling." The bleak and dreary existence of war filters every thread of emotion from the soul leaving only the instinct to survive.

The Pearl Harbor Survivors' Association has many chapters throughout the United States. On December 7 each year the members meet for breakfast, recount their experiences and many of them cry. At 7:55 a.m. the members of the reunion pause for a period of silent prayer. Every fifth year the national meeting is held in Hawaii. As a life member, I attend many of these meetings. The association's motto is—"Remember Pearl Harbor and keep America alert." We take pride in what we have contributed.

17

THE ISLANDS TODAY

Many of these hard won territories, such as Okinawa and Iwo Jima, have been returned to Japanese control. Saipan, on the other hand, is in the process of becoming a United States commonwealth and serves as the capital of the Northern Marianas islands. This new commonwealth will consist of the islands of Rota, Tinian and Saipan and will govern a population of seventeen thousand English speaking citizens. In this largely Roman Catholic country the largest industry is tourism, and we should not be surprised to discover that most of the tourists are Japanese. Indeed, sixty percent of the real estate of Saipan is now owned by the Japanese under land lease arrangements.

Other territories acquired as a direct result of the Pacific campaigns still are administered directly by an agency of the U. S. Government. Guam, the Carolinas and Marshalls are all under the jurisdiction of the Interior Department. Wake Island, on the other hand, is administered by the United States Air Force while Midway is administered by the United States Navy. Many of the other small islands such as Baker and Howland are now uninhabited. The war did not leave our claim to other Pacific territories as clear, however. Our ownership of twenty-five islands located south and southwest of Hawaii is disputed by both the United Kingdom—who claims eighteen of them—and New Zealand—who claims seven.

In March, 1985, on a trip to the Pacific area my wife Frances, and I visited Saipan. We had to change planes on Guam, and were impressed with its progressive development. From the air, we viewed extensive urban development, golf courses, sports complexes, apartment buildings, hotels, and busy Apra Harbor.

The 120 mile flight from Guam to Saipan took us over the islands of Rota and Tinian. In our final approach to Saipan International Airport (formerly Aslito) the landscape became very familiar to me.

We flew over the B-29 runways, the invasion beaches of Saipan and the airport. The runways on the northern point of Tinian Island were almost obscured by scrub growth making it hard to imagine these runways as once being so busy. It was from these runways that the B-29s took off to fire-bomb the cities of Japan and also to drop the atomic bombs.

Gone were the sugar mills and the cane fields, which are now overgrown by scrub trees. Three flags were flying over the terminal: Northern Marianas Commonwealth, Saipan, and the United States of America. A large sign reads "Bienvenido."

I had told my wife that we should use caution in disclosing to the people of Saipan the part I played in the assault of their island, but we soon learned that I was to be looked upon as the rescuer—not the culprit.

The driver who took us to the Hyatt Regency Hotel and later acted as our guide—one Manuel Muna—turned out to be a very distinguished individual. He was a former Senator in their legislature and one of the signers of the Commonwealth Covenant with the United States. Moreover, he had studied on scholarship at New York's Syracuse University, had served with the C.I.A. and had been Washington's contact person for Saipan.

Mr. Muna and his sister had been wounded by naval gunfire during the battle of Saipan. He related that we took them out to our hospital ship where he recovered; however, his sister eventually succumbed to her wounds.

My wife had advised against our visit to Saipan, feeling that the renewal of memories would make me very upset, but I assured her that this would not happen. However, when I knelt beside the grave of Mr. Muna's sister, my compassion for this little innocent six-year-old girl, mortally wounded by our guns, was almost too much to bear. Inscribed on her grave marker was "Amparo D. Muna, Born 4-4-1938, Killed 8-4-1944." When I met a surviving sister, she hugged and kissed me as if I were the prodigal son returning home. This helped to ease some of my pain.

The native Chamorro people are descendants of the original Spanish explorers who traveled to the island with Magellan. To some extent they are all related and readily claim kinship. The majority of the population today is either too young to remember details of the war or was not yet born. I found they were anxious to talk to me and were full of questions about the war. They were a new generation and seemed to know very little about the war that had taken place on their island.

I was equally inquisitive and asked the older Chamorro people some questions of my own, such as: "How did you escape the caves?" One elderly man answered, "A Spanish-speaking person knocked on the door to our cave and asked that all Chamorro people come out. Many did, some did not. Only God knows if any of my missing friends and relatives were buried in their caves." I asked why they were so afraid of the advancing Americans. "The Japanese soldiers told us the the Americans would rape the women and kill the children," was the answer. Now I understood why the children fought so hard when the Americans tried to remove them from the caves. They came out kicking and screaming, and many of the soldiers suffered cracked shins and bruises from these frightened children.

I asked another if he had owned his own home before the war, to which he replied, "Yes, I owned my home then, and after order was restored I rebuilt on my land, as many others did."

I had noticed many foreigners on the island and wondered if they had taken over much of the land. "Only natives can take title to land. Others may make long-term lease agreements," one gentleman was quick to point out.

• An Eyewitness Account •

Since the island relied a great deal on its large tourist trade and the many new jobs it created, I was curious about the effect this new source of income had on the work force. In the past, most of the jobs were in the sugar mills and the cane fields. One man spoke of the new generation with contempt. "Some of my fellow countrymen would rather rest their feet on a desk for fifty cents an hour than do manual labor for ten dollars per hour."

We had another pleasant treat when Dr. and Mrs. Joaquin A. Tenorio, invited us to their home for dinner. They were enthusiastic about the opportunity for firsthand information about the assault on Saipan. Dr. Tenorio is an entomologist for the Marianas Commonwealth and is well versed on the history of Saipan. From him I learned that Saipan exports no products, and the economy relies exclusively on tourism and grants from the United States. They grow fruits and vegetables, and raise chickens and beef for local consumption. Bananas, melons, coconuts, and papayas grow in abundance.

Saipan has tremendous natural landscape attractions which are bathed in tropical splendor. The crystal clear waters, clean white sand, and modern hotels make it an island paradise for honeymooners from Japan. There were few caucasians to be seen on the beaches, so these young couples had no trouble spotting us as visitors from the United States and were quick to ask us to pose with them for pictures.

We learned the Japanese refer to Saipan as their "Pearl Harbor."

Our visit to the historic Japanese prison where American downed flyers were held previous to our assault was a memorable one. Purportedly, Amelia Earhart and her navigator, Fred Noonan, were also detained there. According to local belief, they were brought there from Juliut Atoll in the Marshall Islands. I questioned our guide about this report, and his answers carried a bit of credibility. He stated that the prisoners were moved off the island about six weeks before our assault.

• The POA Defense •

After four days on the Island of Saipan we departed for our return home with a satisfied feeling of "mission accomplished." The Saipanese are a warm and friendly people with gratitude for what our country has done for them since the war. They refer to most dates in history as before or after the war. There is even an imaginary line in their cemetery delineating the burials made before and after the war.

REFLECTIONS

I find it very difficult to lay the blame of the ineffective defense of Pearl Harbor on any one person or group of persons in the United States Forces. We were not at war with anyone—our military forces were by and large in training; the attitude of our government, the populace, and the military was non-belligerent. We were operating under peacetime conservatism, with no funds or preparation to do the things that might have thwarted the attack.

To maintain an adequate peacetime defense against potential enemies takes inestimable amounts of money, and we did not have it appropriated. Our citizens were neither willing to appropriate such funds, nor did they see the need for the nation to arm. We did have ammunition on Oahu, but it was held in storage for protection against corrosion and deterioration.

Quotes from Japanese sources indicated the Pearl Harbor attacking force was ready to abort the mission should they have detected the least evidence that the Americans had even a small capability to defend themselves.

Radar was a relatively new device and was not completely reliable. No central air control existed as we know it today. The need for such a control system did not warrant the cost and manpower.

Our military forces were schooled well in their profession. They had pride and discipline, but were not indoctrinated in the act of war. During duty hours they applied themselves diligently, but after that they were on their own to live somewhat in the style of a civilian. Many high-ranking officers lived off the post because insufficient military housing was available: their absence from the base delayed action during and following the attack.

Esprit de corps is a vital necessity for good military attitude and discipline. The soldier must be so well indoctrinated that his actions and reactions become automatic. The repetition and routine of training necessary to accomplish this is boring, so the Commander must use all means available if he is to maintain morale. Pride and the feeling of being a part of something big is most important. Many things work together to accomplish this. In the main, pomp and show will do it, not only for the soldier, but for the populace as well.

The firing of a weapon is much more awesome at the firing location than at the area of impact; the big boom and rustling of air at the gun site greatly overshadows the crack of the shell burst. For this reason we have an exaggerated opinion of how powerful we are and how destructive our weapons really are.

Our Reserve Officer Training Corps program paid big dividends in World War II by making available to the United States Services thousands of young, professionally-trained officers. They performed well and carried a major share of the load in the conduct of the war. Previously, many of the reserve officers had limited active duty in the administration of the Civilian Conservation Corps which was a big advantage in experience for the officers involved. General E. V. Holmes, Operations Officer, U. S. Army Forces, Pacific Ocean Areas, said, "We could not have fought the war without the help of the reserve officers."

In the Pacific Ocean Areas, our naval air force and the Marines were in the limelight, and rightly so, for carrying the brunt of the attack to the Japanese. In the Southwest Pacific Area the attack fell to Army air and ground forces.

With the receipt of advanced armament and a much-improved radar, our own Army Antiaircraft Artillery units became very effective in combat against the Japanese aircraft; however, they seldom had a chance to prove themselves. During landing operations on the islands antiaircraft artillery was usually kept in a condition of "hold fire," giving way to the defensive capability of the Navy fighter aircraft. By the time the air defense was released to the antiaircraft units, few, if any, attacks by Japanese planes were launched against our island bases. As our area of influence advanced, the Japanese seldom, if ever, attempted a reentry of the war zone, whether they had troops remaining on the islands or not.

The first real opportunity for our Army Antiaircraft Artillery to prove itself came when we loaned General Douglas MacArthur several units for his operation against Leyte in the Philippine Islands. Against the landing of General MacArthur's forces on Leyte, there came hundreds of Japanese aircraft day after day. The tremendous job our Army Antiaircraft Artillery units did in shooting them down soon caused the Japanese to discontinue the attacks. General MacArthur personally lauded the AAA for this feat. An official report from General MacArthur's southwest Pacific headquarters was routed to me. Both the performance and General MacArthur's evaluation of it pleased me very much. I was comforted by the implication that my efforts were somewhat reflected in the good performance of our AAA units.

The professional soldier feels, as his ancestors did, that he is trained and armed with state-of-the-art weapons, and that his proficiency in their use is second to none. He is somewhat like the Olympian, spending years training for the contest that will bring him honor and victory. In combat, however, he soon learns the difference between war and the Olympics. There is no glory on the battlefield. War is ugly; it is death, carnage, and stench. Having survived combat, the experienced soldier is against war forever. General W. T. Sherman of the Civil War era said, "War is hell," and we have yet to find a better phrase to describe it.

There is no other professional society that can closely approximate the military in proficiency, character, morale, discipline, and dedication to the cause. The individual soldier is aware of the dangers in his profession; yet, he is eager to enter into combat. He is prone to challenge a potential foe when the opportunity presents itself. That is the reason the United States

• An Eyewitness Account •

President, through his agencies, must exercise strict and positive control over such encounters. We cannot arm and train our military to fight, and then expect the proper restraint from within the military itself to back away from a challenge. If the decision was his, the combat-wise military man would be the last to commit our nation to war. Yet, if given an assignment, he will comply to the limit of his capacity.

History teaches us that strength is the greatest deterrent to war, yet the strong bully can easily incite the weaker opponent to attack. A snake will make every effort to avoid a person but will stop and fight back if he is tormented. He will do this against the greatest of odds. So will many people.

It is natural for most people to feel they are being mistreated. To counterbalance this, it is necessary that we be more willing to endure suffering than impose suffering on others. The complexity of people is so great that we must give much and expect little in return.

Admiral Chester W. Nimitz was a mild-mannered, low-keyed, and compromising person who performed his duties well. Only such a person could have welded together the combined forces of Army, Navy, Marine, Air Force in World War II so superbly.

I recall an incident following a high level combined conference when a member of the media asked, "How did things go?" and Admiral Nimitz replied with, "Well, let's say it was like the tomcat said when he and the pussy cat emerged with a large litter of kittens—they thought we were fighting. . . ."

Special Services, such as "The Red Cross," "USO" and "The Salvation Army," performed noble roles in their effort to give the military man a touch of "back home" feeling. My heart goes out to the Salvation Army as I remember their late night visits to the lonely guard at his outpost.

CONCLUSION

I do not consider the long way from my humble beginnings to the mountain top as a handicap in my life. On the contrary, I look upon it as a challenge that I have accepted, somewhat like the example which I read about in my primer of the little train climbing a hill saying, "I think I can . . . . I thought I could, I thought I could . . . ." Desire, curiosity, confidence, motivation, determination, and tenacity have been my tools.

"Destiny is not a matter of chance," said William Jennings Bryan, "it is a matter of choice." It was not by accident, nor fate, that on the eve of April 14, 1944 I was a part of an armed force poised to assault the Island of Saipan. Neither was it by accident that I elected to take Advanced Reserve Officers Training in college, maintain my status as a Reserve Officer through correspondence courses, volunteer for temporary active service in the Civilian Conservation Corps, accept active duty in the Armed Services December 1940, volunteer for transfer to the Hawaiian Department in July 1941, nor, on my own volition accompany the Saipan Invasion forces. However so innocent or however so minimal, there are events in my life easily recognizable as part of the infrastructure of "The Making of a World War." A belligerent world provided a medium receptive to someone's lighting the fuse to the fire that became World War II.

Other men may tell their stories and their incidents will be different, but the answers will be the same. The involvement of the Smith family in World War II was not unlike thousands of other families. In keeping with the tradition of the Tennessee Volunteer, each brother, by choice, joined the armed forces as soon as it was feasible to do so.

Times change, men do not. How valid the old axiom is—that you don't have to be a prophet to tell the future. Read the history of the past and apply it to the future—the script is the same. The entrance of the United States into World War II was by choice, not by chance. Our government was impatiently waiting for an occasion like the attack on Pearl Harbor to give us a cogent reason to declare war on Germany and Japan.

The soldier's yearning to fight is a product of his indoctrination, a hate for his enemy, for self-survival, and duty. Also, there is a feeling of obligation to our nation with a debt to be paid for our heritage, and each person has his cross to bear.

Most action beyond the call of duty is not deliberate and heroics occur usually because of mutual concern among buddies for each other. The raising of the flag on Mt. Suribachi on Iwo Jima was not the goal or end within itself and was a ritual not normally highlighted on the battlefield.

People are of ultimate importance—not things. This truth is evident in the nation's wide acceptance of the Vietnam and Pearl Harbor Memorials, which draw attention to those individuals who gave their lives for the cause.

Like Martin Luther King, Jr., I also have a dream. My dream is that some day diplomacy will prevail in the world and there will be no need for wars. Perhaps we should give the teaching of diplomacy as much importance as the teaching of military science and tactics.